FOREWORD

There is only one race—and that race is the human race. It does not matter the color of one's skin or what nationality we are. We are all human souls with a human body. Our souls make us spiritual in nature. God created us in His image—He is spiritual in nature and He is eternal. Our souls are also eternal and will end up in one of two places, heaven or hell. That is why it is so important for each of us to know and understand what every human being's real issue is. This book was written to help us know where our souls will spend eternity.

We can remain in sin, but it is a cruel master. When it pays us off, its wage is death—separation from our Creator forever. In stark contrast, God does not pay wages. He has a free gift to offer—eternal life. There is nothing one can do to earn this gift. If one could earn it, it would not be a gift—it would be wages. Eternal life is just that, eternal. It never ceases.

The basic concept underlying life is UNION. There are three kinds of life mentioned in the Bible. 1. Physical life—union of the soul with the body. 2. Spiritual life—union of the soul with God. 3. Eternal life—eternal union of the soul with God. Jesus said, *My sheep hear My voice and I know them, and they follow Me: and I give them eternal life; and they shall never perish, neither shall any man pluck them out of my hand.* (John 10:27-28 KJV) The gift of God is eternal life. One receives this gift when they believe in Jesus as their personal Savior. Having eternal life, they will never perish.

TABLE OF CONTENTS

Chapter

Lessons

Chapter 1

THE VOID

It was not our choice to be born and to come into this fallen world. We also did not choose our parents. Our lives began at the time of conception. It began the second our earthly father's sperm fertilized our mother's egg. So, for 8 to 10 months, we grew inside our mother's womb. We depended on her for life until the day of our physical birth, when we no longer needed it. That day is called, our date of birth.

There was another beginning which is in Genesis. It says, *In the beginning God*. It refers to the beginning of time, when all things were created. The first man (Adam) and the first woman (Eve) were part of God's creation. They also did not choose to be created. They were created in the image of God. They were created human souls with a human body, making them spiritual in nature, the same as we are today.

Each one of us came into this world under different circumstances. Some of our births were planned by married couples, who knew and loved their Creator. They wanted to raise a family and share their love and the Creator's love. Some of us were birthed by parents because of the lust of the flesh, who did not understand their Creator's love and truth. We all come into this lost and fallen world not understanding our Creator's love and truth, until someone who does takes time to share it with us.

We need to go back to Genesis to understand what happened at the beginning of time. Adam and Eve had a direct and personal relationship with Creator God. They were given the command to not eat the fruit of one tree in the Garden of Eden. They were warned that, if they did, they would surely die. They were tempted by Satan and chose to disobey God. That is when the direct bond with God was broken and everything changed. Man became separated from this relationship, when the first sin was committed by the first couple. The nature of sin was then passed on from generation to generation, leaving this void in everyone's heart.

If we do not understand that we have this void or how this void began, we remain confused. We try to fill the void based on what we know and understand. It's what we don't know that keeps this void empty. We all come into the same fallen and corrupt world and face the same spiritual battle—the battle for our souls. We all have the lust of the flesh, the lies of this world, and Satan himself who wants to kill and destroy. Satan is the father of lies. He wants to keep us from God's truth and His love.

In Psalms 139:13-14 (KJV), David writes these words to His Father God. *For Thou hast possessed me in my mother's womb. I will praise Thee; for I am fearfully and wonderfully made: marvellous are Thy works; and that my soul knoweth right well.*

David knew that he was created by God and that he was fearfully and wonderfully made. He believed in God! He knew in God's eyes that he was valued. We are all uniquely made and uniquely individual. No one is exactly alike. We all have our own DNA, our own set of fingerprints, and our own human soul with a created body.

Many think we can fill this void with worldly things like alcohol, drugs, sex, or other addictions, only to discover that none of these things work. These are all selfish and sinful acts. Most of the time, they make things worse in our lives and for those around us. Throughout recorded human history, compulsive, personally destructive behavior, like addictions, was understood to be a moral failing. This was based on the belief that human beings are moral beings made in the image of God and are responsible for their actions.

Popular opinion about addiction and sinful actions shifted significantly in the 18th and 19th centuries—the result of the views and values expressed by influential proponents of Enlightenment. According to the Age of Enlightenment, reason and science trumped faith and morality. The emphasis was on a purely natural explanation for the world. The idea that human beings were made in the image of God was rejected. Consequently, medical professionals began to examine human behaviors as normal and abnormal. They looked for physiological causes for destructive and personal behavior. They also believed that man evolved and, like animals, human beings possessed an inherent, fundamental survival instinct and would not choose to do anything self-destructive. This led to the belief that addiction must be a disease, because it was considered an abnormal behavior.

Without God, His truth and His morality, men had to come up with excuses to try and explain their behavior. We are great at making excuses, but find it hard to take responsibility. None of us have the physical, mental, or emotional power to free ourselves of our sinful desires. The harder we try on our own strength, the more we fail. If this is true, then what is the answer to overpowering our sinful desires? First, we need to admit we can't do it in our own strength. Second, we need to know a void exists and what the void truly is. Third, we need to be open to the truth of our Creator God. When we are separated from our Creator and have fallen for the lies of this world, then Satan is our spiritual father.

Chapter 2

GOOD COACH/bad coach

We all start out in life on the same team, with the same coach. That's not by choice. The team we are on is a losing team, with a coach that does not want us to win. He will not explain how to play the game and expects us to figure out the rules on our own. Let's use the game of baseball for our example, but it could be any sport. Imagine getting up to bat, not knowing anything about the game or its rules. It's your turn. Someone hands you the bat and says to go to the home plate. Your first thought is, where is home plate and what does home plate mean? Then, what is the purpose of the bat? When I get there what am I supposed to do?

So, you are led out to home plate and are told to swing at the ball, when it is pitched to you. The first ball is pitched—you swing and miss. The second one is pitched—you swing and miss. The third one is pitched—and you swing and miss. The umpire calls, *You're out!* Again, you don't understand what any of this is all about.

Now you're back in the dugout waiting for your next turn. As you observe the other players, you begin to figure that there may be a purpose for this game. But no one explains it to you, because this coach really does not want you to know how to play. So, you keep striking out time after time after time. When you finally do hit the ball, you don't know what to do. Someone yells to run to first base and you think, "Where is that?" So, the ball you hit is thrown to first and the umpire calls you out!

We want help in trying to learn the game, but our coach keeps placing temptations in front of us. He knows our weaknesses, which keeps us out of the game most of the time. At the beginning, we have spectators, parents, brothers, sisters, grandparents, friends, etc. As we continue striking out in this losing game and falling for the temptations our coach places in front of us, our spectators begin to get bored watching us lose. They walk away, knowing they can't help—even when they still love us.

This coach knows we all have the rebellious sin nature we were born with and we have the lust of the flesh within us. He also knows that if he can make us believe life is only about ourselves and our own self-interests, he can continue to lead us away from the game he does not want us to win. He continues to encourage us to believe the lies of this world, because he is the master deceiver. Being on this losing team, we can become discouraged, lose our self-worth, our self-respect, and our dignity. We are in bondage, but our pride and rebellious sin nature keeps us from admitting there must be something better than this. There must be another team and coach somewhere that wants us to win. I know I did not choose this team nor this coach, that was beyond my control.

All the temptations our existing coach places in front of us (that we fall for) may make us feel good for a while, but we find they are temporary. They end up being all about self. These temptations may bring us temporary enjoyment, but they keep us out of the game. At the time, we don't care about the damage to ourselves and those around us or the ones involved with us during these actions. We keep trying to put on a good face, trying to make those around us believe we are OK—but inside we hurt so deeply, not knowing where to turn. We know deep down inside of us something is missing and something is not right being on this losing team.

???(The Void)????

Good News! There is another team we can join with a different coach. He is not a coach that recruits players for His team. When we choose to join His team, He welcomes us with open arms and a loving smile. He already knows everything about us and all the struggles and mistakes we've made, while playing on the losing team. He knows we have not been taught the rules of the game or how to play the game. This Coach will take all the time in the world to work with us, as long as we come to Him and ask for His help. You see, He loves us unconditionally and wants the best for our lives. He will never tempt us nor forsake us. When we are ready to step to the plate, He will teach us how to stand properly, how to hold the bat, and to keep our eyes on the ball. As He hands us the bat, He tells us this bat is carved out of the Cross in which He gave His life for us and paid the price for our past sins, while playing on the losing team.

One of the first things He tells us, is we need to place our faith in Him—not in ourselves, not in others, and not in the things of this world, for all things in this world are temporary. He is eternal. He also tells us the same about hope. Then He tells us if we really want to be on His team and want to learn how to play the game, we are to love Him with all our heart, mind, and soul. We are also to love the other players (neighbors) as ourselves.

He then tells us that now, when we step up to the plate, we will begin to hit singles, doubles, and sometimes triples. But if you really want to start hitting home runs, we need to tell Him all the things we did when we fell for the temptations the old coach dangled in front of us and ask for forgiveness. He calls it *repentance*. He then says that

He took the punishment that we so rightly deserved on that cross. He paid the price in full for each one of us so, we could be on His team and not have to carry our past with us.

Now, on this winning team, we have the Owner (God), the Owner's Son (Jesus, our Coach), and His Assistant (the Holy Spirit). Our new Coach, Jesus, tells us it is very important that we deny ourselves daily, to pick up our cross (the bat), and to follow Him—because He is the Way, the Truth, and the Life. No one can come to the Father, except through Him. He does not say that any particular church or religion is the way. He says He is the only way to His Father God.

He also warns us that the old coach will do everything in his power to put temptations in front of us and try to get us back on his team. The old coach does not want us to win. But the Coach's Assistant, the Holy Spirit, will come alongside us and fill us with His strength to fight against these temptations—if we allow Him to do so.

Our new Coach also tells us about a Book that has been written with the *Basic Instructions Before Leaving Earth* in it. It is better known as the BIBLE. In this book we find the instructions and rules for the game. This is the best-selling book of all time. Read and study the Bible, because it is His Story. If we really want to develop a personal relationship with God, we need to spend time together. We all have the same choice to make—we can stay on the losing team with the old coach who wants us to fail, or we can join the new team with the new Coach who wants us to win this game of life.

When we observe all of God's Creation, we see everything has a purpose, from the stars in the sky, the moon, and our sun, even down to the smallest insect. All animals on land, all fish in the sea, and all the various plants and trees have a purpose. If we can see and understand this, then we, as part of His creation, have a purpose.

We will never know or understand this purpose while playing on the wrong team and listening to the wrong coach.

Winning Team Membership

➤ I hereby declare I no longer belong to the team I was born into and denounce my old coach. I know he does not want me to win and has placed temptation after temptation in my path. This old coach was no help at all in teaching me how to play the game.

➤ It is my desire to join this new team with a Coach who welcomes me with open arms and a loving smile. I openly confess I do not know or understand the rules of how to play. I ask for forgiveness of my actions in following the temptations placed before me, while playing on the losing team.

➤ I accept Jesus as my Coach from this day forward, knowing His Father is the Owner of this team and the Holy Spirit is Jesus' Assistant Coach. He will teach me and help me learn the rules from the Bible – *B*asic *I*nstructions *B*efore *L*eaving *E*arth. I commit to be open to the Owner's TRUTH written in His Book.

On this day, month, and year of the Lord, _____,
I surrender my will and humble myself to Him, being committed to follow my new Coach and His teachings.

_____

Signature

Chapter 3

STORY OF TWO POEMS

The first poem was sent to me via email, after I had visited my son who was in the hospital in Lincoln, NE. He had attempted suicide—at that time, he was in his 40s. He had been addicted to drugs since the age of 15. Our greatest fear as parents was he would not live to the age of 30, because of the choices he had made.

When I returned home from Lincoln, after making sure he was going to be alright, I was checking my email when this poem called, *Bad Coach*, appeared. As I read it, tears began to run down my cheeks, because this was our biggest fear for our son. I read through it several times and the tears kept flowing. I then printed it and kept reading through the words. I began to see and feel the evil and darkness of this addiction. As I read it over again and again, I started changing some of the words to give it a different message. When I was finished, I realized that evil and darkness can be changed to goodness and light. I titled this poem, *Good Coach*. Here are the two poems.

Bad Coach

The story goes like this. A young girl, who was in jail for drug charges, was addicted to meth. She wrote this while in jail. As you read it you will see that she fully grasped the horrors of the drug. Not long after being released, she was found dead with the needle still in her arm.

BAD COACH

I dismantle homes, I rip families apart,
I take your children, and that's just the start.
I'm more expensive than diamonds, more costly than gold,
The misery I bring is a sight to behold.

If you want me, remember, I can be found,
I live all around you, in schools and in town.
I live with the wealthy, I live with the poor.
I live up the street and maybe next door.

In a lab I can be made, but it's not like you think,
I can be made in your kitchen, right in the sink.
I've been found in your child's closet, and even in the woods,
If this scares you to death—well, it certainly should.

Many names I do have, but there's one you know best.
I'm sure you've heard of me, my name's crystal meth.
My power is consuming, try me and you'll see,
but if you do, you may never break free.

Just try me once and I might let you go,
But try me twice, and I'll own your soul.
My power will possess you, you'll steal and you'll lie.
But you'll do what you have to, just to get high.

The crimes you'll commit for my narcotic charms
will be worth the pleasure you'll feel in your arms.
You'll lie to your mother and you'll steal from your dad.
When you see their tears, you should feel sad.

You will forget your morals and how you were raised,
I'll be your conscience, I'll teach you my ways.
I separate kids from parents and parents from kids,
I turn people from God, and I'm glad that I did.

I will take everything from you, your looks and your pride,
I will always be with you, right by your side.
I will take everything—your family, your home,
your friends, your money, then you'll be alone.

I will take and take, 'til you have nothing more to give,
when I'm finished with you, you will be lucky to live.
If you try me, be warned, this is no game.
if given a chance I will drive you insane.

I will ravish your body. I will control your mind.
I will own you completely. Your soul will be mine.
The nightmares I'll give you while sleeping in bed,
the voices you'll hear from inside your head.

The sweats, the shakes, the visions you'll see,
I want you to know, these are gifts from me.
But then it will be too late, and you will know in your heart,
that you are mine and we shall not part.

You will regret that you tried me, they always do,
you came to me, not I to you.
You knew this would happen, many times you were told,
but you challenged my strength and chose to be bold.

You could have said "no," and just walked away,
If you could live that day over, now what would you say?
I will be your master, you will be my slave,
I will go with you, when you go to the grave.

Now that you have met me, what will you do?
Will you try me or not? It is all up to you.
I can bring you more problems than words can tell,
come take my hand, let me lead you to hell.

This poem portrays the evil of drugs, where many who become addicted end up dead. They did not understand the void we all start out in life with and how we got that void. They live in bondage and don't know how to escape, so they try ways of this world to fill this empty feeling. This next poem was written by changing some of the words in this poem to give it a different meaning.

GOOD COACH

I build homes, I keep families together.
I give you your children—that's a gift that matters.
I'm more expensive than diamonds, more costly than gold,
the happiness I bring is a sight to behold.

If you need Me, remember, I am easily found.
I live all around you, in schools and in town.
I live with the wealthy, I live with the poor,
I live up the street, and maybe next door.

I was born to save you, no matter what you think,
It's a choice to be made, as quick as a blink.
I'm in your child's closet, and even in the woods,
If you want eternal life, you certainly should.

I have many names, but there's one that pleases,
I'm sure you've heard of Me, My name is Jesus!
My power is awesome. Try Me, you'll see;
but if you do, expect to be free.

Just try Me once, and you might let go,
But try Me twice, and I will own your soul.
The time you commit to My spiritual charms,
Will be worth the pleasure as you rest in My arms.

You will love your mother, and respect your dad;
when you see their eyes, you will feel so glad.
And you'll remember your morals and how you were raised,
I'll be your conscience, I'll teach you My ways.

I give kids to parents and parents to kids,
I turn people from Satan and forgive what they did.
I have given you everything, your looks and your stride,
I'll be with you always, right by your side.

I have given you everything—your family, your home,
Your friends, your money—you are never alone.
I will give and give, 'til you learn how to give—
when I am finished with you, you'll know how to live.

If you try Me, be warned, this is no game,
If given the chance, I'll keep you sane.
I will refresh your body and peace of mind,
I'll own you completely, your soul will be Mine.

The dreams I will give you while sleeping in bed,
My voice you will hear from inside your head.
The hope, the love, and the peace you will see,
I want you to know, these are all gifts from Me.

It is never too late and you'll know in your heart,
that you are Mine and we shall not part.
You'll be thankful you trusted in Me, they always do,
You came to Me, and I came for you.

You knew this would happen, many times you were told,
but you trusted My power and chose to be bold.
You could have said, "No" and just walked away,
but you placed your trust in Me. WOW. What a wonderful day!

I'll be your Master, you've come to serve,
I'll always be with you, even if you lose your nerve.
Now that you have met Me, what will you do?
Will you trust in Me or not? It's all up to you.
I will give you a life you may never fathom.
Come take my hand and let Me lead you to Heaven.

You see, we are all products of our past, but we do not have to remain slaves to our past. We also need to know who owns our soul. The poem, *BAD COACH*, displays the darkness and evil that comes from the use of drugs in trying to fill the void. The poem, *GOOD COACH*, displays the light and good of having the void filled with Jesus. Either we remain in bondage, trying to fill this void on our own—or we surrender to the truth and wisdom from above to fill this void. There really is nothing between the two options.

You may wonder how things turned out for our son. He is now in his 50s. He and his lady friend stopped using drugs. They have been smoke-free for several months. It is all due to the power of prayer, plus, being sick and tired of being in bondage. All the time we were raising our children, we did not fully understand this void or the reason for it. We were believers in God and Jesus, but we never made the choice to follow Jesus and make Him the Lord of our lives—nor did we have a personal relationship with Him. We were never encouraged to read the Bible, God's Word.

We now have the best relationship a father and son can have. A couple of years ago I received this text message from him on Father's Day.

Dad, you are the best!!!! When I was young, you married my mother, adopted me and my sister, and started growing our great family. You have worked so hard to constantly improve yourself for the best of our family. With a lot of days and nights you always strove to be your best. While it wasn't easy, you raised me the best you could, and I love you for it. The man I am today is because of the man you have always been. Your love, compassion, and faith pulled me literally out of hell. Your hard work and dedication to our family will never be forgotten, and your legacy will be with us for generations. You've made my mother happy and did your best. You show dignity and class in everything you do. I wish I could be one tenth of the man you are. I love you more than life, Dad. Even though I can't be there today, I just want you to know how important you are to me and how loved you are. I love you, your son. Oh yeah, HAPPY FATHERS DAY!

Praise God!

You don't think this didn't touch my heart in a special way?

The power of prayer!

Chapter 4

FILLING THE VOID

The void is our separation from our Creator God. We long for that relationship—the way it started with the first man (Adam) and first woman (Eve). God knew that none of us had the physical, mental, or emotional strength to deal with our sin and our sin nature. In His infinite wisdom, He sent His one and only Son to be the sacrifice for us. Jesus took on Himself the sins of this world. He took the punishment and was nailed to a wooden cross. He took what we deserved. He took our place.

It is not a particular church or religion that saves us from our sins, it is a personal relationship with Jesus. Placing our total faith and trust in Him and Him alone fills this void we all long for. He tells us in John 14:6, (KJV). *Jesus saith unto him, I am the way, the truth, and the life: no man cometh unto the Father, but by me.* We need to admit we are not strong enough to fight the spiritual battle we all face each day. The real question is, are we weak enough to allow God's Holy Spirit to fight this battle for us? That's called surrender. He asks us to love Him with all our hearts, with all our minds, and with all our soul.

When we truly love someone, we **want to** be obedient and no longer feel **we have** to be obedient. So how does one acquire this personal relationship? It is acquired the same way we build a personal relationship with anyone— spending time to get to know them. God in His infinite wisdom gave us His Living Word found in the Bible (Basic Instructions Before Leaving Earth). This is the only place where we can find godly wisdom and truth. It is the truth that sets us free.

According to the 1828 Webster's Dictionary, wisdom is defined: *In Scripture theology, wisdom is true religion; godliness; piety; the knowledge and fear of God, and sincere and uniform obedience of His commands. This is wisdom from above. The wisdom of this world, mere human erudition; or the carnal policy of men, their craft and artifices in promoting temporal interests called fleshly wisdom.* This is wisdom from sinful man.

All things of this world are temporary and will not last forever. Even our human bodies are temporary and will someday return to dust, but our souls are eternal and will live forever. If the truths of our Creator God and His wisdom are found in the Bible, then why do we look to this fallen world and man's wisdom for answers? If it is true that Jesus is the only One who can fill this void we are all born with, then why wouldn't we want to develop a personal relationship with Him—so we can call our Creator God our Spiritual Father? What else has worked?

In the book of Romans, (KJV) the Apostle Paul wrote in Chapter 1:20-21, *For the invisible things of Him from creation of the world are clearly seen, being understood by the things that are made, even His eternal power and God head; so that they are without excuse: because that, when they knew God, they glorified him not as God, neither were thankful; but became vain in their imaginations, and their foolish hearts were darkened.*

In Romans 3:22-26, (KJV) *Even the righteousness of God which is by faith of Jesus Christ unto all and upon all them that believe; for there is no difference; For all have sinned, and come short of the glory of God; being justified freely by his grace through the redemption that is in Christ Jesus: whom God hath set forth to be a propitiation through faith in his blood, to declare His righteousness for the remission of sins that are past through the forbearance of God; to declare, I say, at this time His righteousness: that He might be just, and the justifier of him which believeth in Jesus.*

Paul makes one thing clear in the first three chapters of Romans—all people are guilty before God and deserving of His judgment. Not one person alive can do anything to earn God's favor. How then do we find salvation? Paul says that we are justified by God's grace. The word *justification* refers to the act by which God, the righteous judge, declares guilty sinners not guilty. God freely gives us this forgiveness—it is not something we earn.

Must a person participate in any religious ritual to be saved from the penalty of sin? Paul teaches that all people are made right with God by faith in Jesus Christ, apart from anything they might do to win God's favor. If we want to be a person of God, remember that neither rituals nor good deeds will help us win God's favor. Salvation is not based on something we do for God. It involves accepting what God has already done for us through His Son Jesus the Christ.

Romans 5:1-5 (KJV) says, *Therefore being justified by faith, we have peace with God through our Lord Jesus Christ: by whom also we have access by faith into this grace wherein we stand and rejoice in hope of the glory of God. And not only so, but we glory in tribulations also: knowing that tribulation worketh patience; and patience experience; and experience, hope: and hope maketh not ashamed; because the love of God is shed abroad in our hearts by the Holy Ghost which is given unto us.*

Chapter 5

SIN

(Selfish Individualized Non-since)

The 1828 Webster's Dictionary explains sin to be *the voluntary departure of a moral agent from a known rule of rectitude of duty, prescribed by God; any voluntary transgression of divine law or violation of a divine command.*

God determines morality and truth based on His authority—sinful man has no authority over what is moral or immoral. Every sin any of us commit is when we are thinking only of ourselves. Sin always takes us further than we want to go, keeps us longer than we want to stay, and costs us more than we want to pay.

Sin is being disobedient to God's authority and to what He says is true. We were given the ability and the free will to make choices. The world wants us to believe that addictions are a disease, not a personal choice. The myth that addiction is a disease has serious implications, because it separates people from their addiction. If it is true that addiction is a disease, then it is not a moral problem nor one of personal responsibility—and will power and self-control have no place in recovery.

Since ideas matter, it is important to correct this false belief, so we share the truth. A disease is something you have—addiction is something you do. This is not a minor distinction, but the major difference separating human behavior from a medical condition. A person has cancer, for example, but an addict does a particular thing. Behavior is not disease, but rather the voluntary, free-will action of human beings.

While addiction is clearly a choice, there are undoubtedly reasons why a person chooses to abuse alcohol or drugs. However, a reason is not justification. As moral beings, we are responsible for our actions and the resulting behavior. Those behaviors and choices resulting in terrible consequences are considered a moral failing. This may cause us to feel uncomfortable.

We do not like to think of addiction in terms of right and wrong. Since addiction often involves self-destructive behavior resulting in terrible physical and emotional pain, some argue it cannot be a choice. This is also incorrect. We are free-will moral beings. Our inherent capacity to choose also means we can do self-destructive things. We can either choose to do the morally sensible thing or continue to live in sin.

The reality is addiction is a sinful, personal choice. It is not only personally destructive, but it also impacts others who are close to the problem. It rips apart families and causes extraordinary pain in communities struggling to deal with drug related crime and poverty. Until we recognize that addiction is a personal choice, it will continue to spread without restraint, creating a society of victims who are hoping to excuse their sinful behavior.

When we look at this definition of recovery, we are all in recovery as we enter this fallen world. RECOVERY is the entire process of healing from the painful effects of dysfunctional behavior. In the larger sense, everything in Christian ministry is recovery. We may think of it this way—God created us with a glorious purpose. Sin warped and twisted this purpose. Recovery is the process of restoring what sin has taken away.

Salvation is a gift from God for all of us to receive, if we so choose. If salvation is a gift, what's to keep us from sinning? Why not sin? Because as a believer and follower of Christ, we are spiritually identified with Jesus in His death and resurrection. And because sin has no power over Jesus, it has no power over us or over those who are united with Him.

So then, are followers of Jesus free from sinful appetites? No, although we wish we could be. Those appetites no longer have unbridled power over us. Think of sin and its effects as a motorcycle with a disconnected chain. The engine (sin) still has great power, but it can't turn the wheels (action). Similarly, for followers of Jesus, the chain that drives our sinful activity has been disconnected. Our sinful motor is still there and at times we may re-engage the chain. But the more we realize we are liberated from sin's power, the more we find ourselves living free of its appetites. If we have accepted Jesus' resurrection, we no longer have to pray for power over sin. We already have that. Instead, pray we will utilize the power we have. Ask for the grace we need to stand in the freedom Jesus has given us.

No matter how long we have known Jesus Christ, we will still feel sin trying to pull us away from God. But that does not mean defeat is inevitable. Jesus not only promises us victory—He assures it. Just as the principle of sin is that sin always pulls us down—so the principle of the Spirit of life is that the Spirit always lifts us up. Whenever we are tempted with sin, we need to turn to God's Spirit and ask for His help, to lift us above the power of sin.

Chapter 6

CONFESSION

Psalm 38:18 (KJV)—*For I will declare mine iniquity; I will be sorry for my sin.*

Romans 10:9 (KJV)—*That if thou shalt confess with thy mouth the Lord Jesus, and shalt believe in thine heart that God hath raised him from the dead, thou shalt be saved.*

James 5:16 (KJV)—*Confess your faults one to another, and pray one for another, that ye may be healed. The effectual fervent prayer of a righteous man availeth much.*

1 John 1:9 (KJV)—*If we confess our sins, He is faithful and just to forgive us our sins, and to cleanse us from all unrighteousness.*

Some of us misunderstand 1 John 1:9. We think confessing purchases forgiveness. The point of the passage is that God is faithful and just. Our forgiveness had already been paid for at the cross. Confession enables us to experience what God has already granted. Confession is a means by which we can experience our forgiveness, not obtain it.

The fact God has forgiven us does not mean we automatically experience that forgiveness. We still may be in slavery to feelings of guilt and shame. We desperately need to experience His forgiveness, because deep-seated feelings of shame fuel our addictions. When we bring our hidden guilt and shame into the open (with someone who has shown he or she can be trusted), we somehow find it easier to receive forgiveness and experience freedom from the burden of our sins.

The more we experience forgiveness, the more we will be able to forgive those who have hurt us. If we are honest with ourselves, we may see that failing to forgive results from believing we are morally superior—that as a victim, we have the right to go on accusing, despising, and denouncing those we refuse to forgive. Be sure to understand, our confession does not make us forgiven. We are forgiven, because Jesus died to pay for our sins. Confession is a means for us to experience forgiveness, not a way to obtain it.

All too often, we play the game of penance, so we can feel forgiven. Once convicted of a sin, we might plead with God for forgiveness. Then we are depressed for a couple of days, just to show we are sorry and deserve to be forgiven. We attempt to pay for our sins by feeling bad. But we cannot earn forgiveness by punishing ourselves. Confession simply involves applying the forgiveness we already have in Jesus. Accepting His forgiveness allows us to move on with the Lord and joyfully serve Him.

Many of us immediately feel shame when we hear the word *sin*. Please understand when the Bible talks of sin, it refers to the spiritual condition affecting every human being. God hates sin, because sin harms the people He loves. Pretending we have no sin is shameful. Admitting our sin is not shameful. Confessing our sin is honest and courageous. When we confess our sin openly to God, we agree with what God already knows about us—and God will forgive us.

Are we trusting in our own abilities to earn acceptance with God, or are we trusting in the death of Jesus to pay for our sins? Are we trusting in what we can accomplish, or are we trusting in the resurrection of Jesus to give us new life? Trusting in Jesus does not guarantee we will be delivered instantly from our problems in life. It is a process. It means we are forgiven and restored to a relationship with Him. We will receive His unconditional love and acceptance, as well as His strength and wisdom, as we continue to grow in recovery.

We must also repent of all our sins we knowingly are committing or are involved in. Repent means we are to *turn from and go the other way.* Many sins like addictions, pornography, gambling, homosexuality, lusting, etc., cannot be conquered in our own strength. We need the help of the Holy Spirit to help win these battles. This is why Jesus tells us in Scripture that we must deny ourselves, pick up our cross daily and follow Him. Denying oneself is to surrender our will to His will. Remember, every sin any of us ever commit (or will ever commit) is when we are only thinking of self.

In John 8:34-36 (KJV), Jesus says, *Verily verily, I say unto you, Whosoever committeth sin is the servant of sin. And the servant abideth not in the house for ever: but the Son abideth ever. If the Son therefore shall make you free, ye shall be free indeed.* Without our total faith in Jesus, we remain a slave to sin. Freedom from the power of sin is a freedom to know and to serve God. That freedom is not found through any religious activity. True freedom comes through a personal relationship with the One who is the embodiment of the true path to salvation—Jesus Christ. When the gift of Jesus lives within a person, He liberates that person from enslavement to sin and death. We have all sinned and struggled with sin. We know its tyrannical hold. We have felt its tight, vise-like grip on our soul. By holding to His teaching and through the power of the Holy Spirit, we can become His true disciples in thought, word, and deed.

Our flesh and the Spirit are totally opposed to each other. The one we allow to dominate will take charge and produce its own fruit. The solution to the urges of the flesh lies in being under the control of the Spirit's power. Galatians 5:16 (KJV)—*This I say then, walk in the Spirit. And ye shall not fulfil the lust of the flesh.* It is a moment-by-moment dependence and faith in the Spirit's power. We must choose to act in His will, to benefit from the Spirit's enablement. If we struggle in our own strength, we will fail. There is no secret formula to make the Spirit's power available. It is simply a reliance on the Holy Spirit to help when tempted.

Chapter 7

HEAVEN, WILL YOU BE THERE?

There is a lot of uncertainty with many people about knowing for sure if they will go to heaven when they die. Most people, when asked the question, *Will you go to heaven when you die?* really don't know. Some answers you may hear are the following: I don't know. I'm working on it. I have no idea. I'm not sure. Many say they believe in Jesus and heaven, but do not know for sure if they will be there. How do you answer this question?

Most are sure about a lot of things, yet they do not know if heaven will be their eternal home. When we plan a trip or vacation, we know our destination before we venture out. There is a lot of misunderstanding in what one must do to attain eternal life in heaven. Some might say that you need to live a good life, obey the Ten Commandments, join a church and attend regularly, love your fellow man, be baptized or confirmed, follow the teaching of Jesus. These are good answers, but they all reflect that eternal life in heaven has to be earned.

Scripture is clear—we cannot earn or win our way to heaven. Eternal life in heaven is a free gift from God. We are not rewarded for what we have done or tried to do. It is by God's grace alone, in our faith alone, and in Christ alone. It is not from ourselves. It is God's precious gift of His Son, Jesus. The question is, will we freely receive this wonderful gift?

When we believe we have to work to earn our way into heaven, how would we ever know if we have done enough to deserve heaven? None of us are good enough to measure up to God's perfect standards. It would be prideful if we said that we knew we were going to heaven by our works. Scripture tells us we cannot be good enough, we cannot work our way to heaven, and we don't need to! Jesus opened the way to heaven for us. Anyone can qualify, no matter what we have done or how bad we were.

Scripture also tells us that no one will be declared righteous in God's sight by observing the law. Rather, it is through the law that we become aware of sin. The righteousness from God, apart from the law, has been known. This righteousness from God comes through our faith in Jesus Christ to all who believe.

God sent His only Son to pay the price for our sins—yours and mine—by His death on the cross. Having completely paid our sin penalty, He rose from the dead and offers eternal life in heaven for you and me as a gift. By understanding our need for a divine Savior and by accepting His payment for our sins, the matter of our eternal destiny is immediately resolved.

Chapter 8

WHY IS THERE EVIL AND WHY DOES GOD ALLOW IT?

John 3:19 (KJV)—*And this is the condemnation, that light is come into the world, and men loved darkness rather than light, because their deeds were evil.*

With all the murders, terrorist attacks, looting, anger, lies and hate in this world, it is natural to ask, Why does God allow such evil acts? If God is so loving, great, and good, why does He allow humans to hurt each other?

There is an answer—it is both our greatest blessing and our worst curse. It is our capacity and ability to make choices. We are created with a free will and a void. We are made in our Creator's image. We have been given the freedom to decide how we act and the ability to make moral choices. This ability sets us apart from the animals. It is also the source of so much pain in the world. We are all capable of making selfish, self-centered, and even evil choices, without the truth of God. When this happens, people get hurt.

We know that all sin is selfishness. We tend to do what we want and not do what God tells us to do. Sin always hurts others, not just ourselves. Yes, God could have eliminated all evil from the world, by simply removing our ability to choose. By taking away our ability to choose, evil would vanish. He could have made us puppets on strings that He pulls, but God does not want us to be puppets or slaves. He wants us to be obedient creatures, who freely and voluntarily choose to love Him and each other. Love is not genuine, if there is no other option. Having the love of Jesus in our hearts, allows us to love others.

God could have kept the terrorists from completing their suicide missions and the murders that take place every day. He could have short circuited their ability to choose their own will instead of His. But to be fair, God would also have to do that to all of us. While you and I are not terrorist or killers, we do hurt others with our own selfish decisions and actions.

In a world where people have the ability to make choices, God's will is seldom done. Doing our own will is more common and easier. We should not blame God for all of the tragedies. Blame the people who ignore what God says to do, *Love your neighbor as yourself.* Our love of others can only be unconditional when Jesus fills the void within our hearts.

In heaven, God's will is perfect—there will be no sorrow, pain, or evil there. We currently live in a fallen imperfect world. We must choose to do God's will every day, because it is not automatic. In the Lord's Prayer, Jesus tells us to pray, *Thy will be done on earth, as it is in heaven.* We are much more interested in pleasing ourselves than in pleasing the One who created us. We must look to God and His Word for comfort, direction, and answers to our questions. We must humble ourselves and admit that we often choose to ignore what God wants us to do. We were made for a relationship with our Creator God—and He waits for us to choose Him. He is ready to guide, comfort, and direct us through this life on earth.

Chapter 9

RELIGION VS. RELATIONSHIP

Have you ever wondered where you would be attending church services today, if your parents had been raised in one of the other churches or religions? We all tend to follow in our parent's footsteps, when it comes to what church we attend. Their beliefs and faith affect our own. Right or wrong, that is the way it is. So, who is to say any one religion or church is superior over the other in its beliefs and teachings?

Picture a row of bowling balls on a long rack. All the balls on the rack are black except the one in the middle. The one in the middle is white. On the black balls are the names of all the world religions. Inside each ball is the doctrinal beliefs of each religion. On the bottom of each of the black balls are two letters—DO. You need to DO based on doctrinal beliefs.

On the white ball is the name JESUS. Inside this ball is the Holy Bible, God's written word to us. On the bottom of this ball, there are four letters—DONE! Our part is to accept His truth and His love, to love Him and be obedient. Salvation is by His grace alone and our faith is in Christ alone.

SEEK AND YOU WILL FIND!

The ten lessons which follow, are designed to help you seek God and find Him. By taking time to study through the lessons, you will begin your journey to develop a personal relationship with your Savior, Jesus Christ.

Some of you may never have opened a Bible—or even own one. I encourage you to purchase a Bible, if you do not have one, and begin this life changing journey. I personally use the King James Bible version. Many people own one or more Bibles, but seldom spend time reading or studying it.

It has been said, if everyone in America opened their Bibles at the same time, there would be a dust storm that would last for several days. Lots of Bibles lay around collecting dust, because people do not open them.

Take your time as you work through each lesson. The lessons are designed to build on one another and to help you grow in your walk with God's truth and His love.

Lesson ONE

UNDERSTANDING GOD, IN THE MIDST OF CHAOS

Welcome to this exciting Bible study. There is a specific reason this Bible study is entitled *Seeking God and Finding Him*. There is nothing more fulfilling in this world than to search out the Creator of the Universe. You have probably heard stories about adults, who were adopted at a young age, that have pursued information regarding their natural parents. We all have the desire to know more about our upbringing and origin. This same idea is also true when it comes to the origin of the human race. Who did you ultimately come from?

For centuries, philosophers, scientists, and theologians have debated the origins of man and the ultimate creator of the universe. Every person has a unique desire to investigate, speculate, and think about why he/she was placed on this earth. Is there real purpose in life—or are we here by chance? The Bible declares that every living person in this world is uniquely created by a personal and loving God. God created you and knows you far better than you even know yourself. He wants nothing more than for you to genuinely know and love Him. God says that He will reveal Himself to anyone that truly seeks Him out.

Look up the following verses and record the portion of the verse pertaining to the subject. If you are not familiar with where these books of the Bible are located, go to your table of contents. (OT) will mean Old Testament and (NT) will mean New Testament.

1. Matthew 7:7-8 (NT)

_____
_____
_____
_____

2. Proverbs 8:17 (OT)

_____
_____
_____
_____

God delights and gives promises to those who seek Him. Many times, God allows things to happen in one's life, both good and bad, to cause an individual to seek Him. From our perspective, it may seem we are doing all the seeking, but in reality, God is also seeking us.

3. Luke19:10 (NT)

_____
_____
_____
_____

As we will see in the upcoming lessons, every person is born lost and without God. Because of sin, it is not our natural inclination to seek God and love Him. In and of ourselves, we are lost and without God, but in his mercy and love he seeks us. He desires to save that which is lost. We never come to understand this, however, until we come to the point of seeking Him and looking into the Bible. The amazing thing is, when we finally do seek after God and look at what

He has communicated in His word, we find our loving and intimate Creator.

4. Is there anything in your life, either positive or negative, you would say has caused you to pause and realize you need to seek God in your life, or has caused you to realize God has been seeking you?

_____

_____

_____

_____

Remember God's promise: "Those who seek Me, find Me." Perhaps God has allowed you to experience something in your life, to make you realize that you cannot do it alone. We are all in need of God, our Creator.

Confusion, in the Midst of Relativism

You may or may not be aware of the philosophy of our current culture. We live in what is called a relativistic or post-modern society. As you seek God, it is important for you to know the cultural context you are in. There are four basic means of authority, when it comes to knowledge and beliefs. Everything we believe to be true is derived from one of these four sources of authority: 1) reason, 2) tradition, 3) experience, 4) the Bible. Obviously, we use all four to help shape our knowledge and beliefs about the world.

We believe that two plus two equals four, because it is reasonable and logical (reason). There are certain things we believe simply because our parents, church, or school taught them to us (tradition). We believe that drinking coffee that is too hot will burn our tongue, because we have felt it (experience). We believe Jesus Christ walked this earth 2000 years ago, because that is what the Bible teaches

(Bible). Therefore, we use all four sources of authority to develop our belief system.

However, many times two or more sources of authority render opposing conclusions on a subject or issue. Then a person is forced to choose one source of authority, usually the one placed at the top. At different points in history, cultures have placed the emphasis on different sources of authority. For example, during the 15th and 16th century, tradition was a stronghold in society. During the Enlightenment period of the 17th and 18th century, reason was set as the supreme court of authority.

5. From the four sources of authority that were just given, evaluate these four statements. Write down the final source of authority being used.

a) I was always taught that as long as you love people and are a good person you will go to heaven—and that is what I believe.

_____

_____

_____

_____

b) The Bible says that God has no beginning and no ending; therefore, that is what I believe.

_____

_____

_____

_____

c) It does not make sense to me that God would create people and then judge many of them to hell. Therefore, I cannot believe this is true.

_____

_____

_____

_____

d) I will not believe in the God of the Bible, unless He personally appears to me or performs a miracle before my eyes. The way I live right now feels right for me."

_____

_____

_____

_____

In our day, experience has become the dominating source of authority. In a relativistic society, no one has a right to tell anyone he is wrong. There are no absolutes—everything is relative. What is right and wrong for you is relative to your experience. What is right and wrong for me is relative to my experience. No longer is there an outside source to man's existence to render things right and wrong. Man and his experience is now the final judge. This is the difference between a man-centered world and a God-centered world. This secular, humanistic mindset has taken our current society captive. People today generally do what is right in their own eyes.

6. Record 2 Timothy 3:16 (NT)

_____

_____

_____

_____

In what ways do you think this verse opposes the relativistic mindset?

_____

_____

This passage says Scripture is God-breathed, not man-breathed. The Scriptures, coming from God, are intended to teach, rebuke, correct, and train. God created this world and whatever He says authoritatively distinguishes right from wrong. Where there is a relativistic mindset, however, there is chaos. If there are no absolutes, and no one can make universal statements about right and wrong, think about the logical conclusion—morality is based solely on the opinion of each person's own feelings. "If I want to have an affair on my spouse, who are you to say I am wrong. I decide what is right and wrong for me." This reasoning can be given to verify anyone's actions. In this system of thought, nothing outside of man renders right from wrong.

When someone admits the human race has been created by God, however, and God has communicated to us through the Bible, you have someone outside of man determining right from wrong. This is exactly why God has not left us on our own in this world, but has spoken to us in His Word. When men are left on their own to form their own belief system, one only needs to watch the nightly news to see the results. The world is filled with rebellion and moral chaos. We live in this relativistic society where everyone rationalizes their own behavior, regardless of how evil and wrong it is. *If it feels right to me, who are you to say it is wrong?* When men turn to the Bible and seek to know God, the results are as drastic in the opposite direction. In the week to come, notice the relativistic minds people in our society display. Think about how it has affected your belief system, perhaps without you ever even knowing it.

The Attributes of God

In order to understand God, we must understand His attributes and characteristics. The Bible is God's revelation. God chose to reveal Himself to man through the means of His written Word. Let's look at a few ways in which God describes Himself to us.

7. God is holy, which means He is different than anything else in all of creation—and, He is pure. His holiness speaks of His separateness and uniqueness. Exodus 15:11 (OT)

_____

_____

_____

_____

Habakkuk 1:13 (OT) (first half of verse)

_____

_____

_____

_____

8. God is love. Jeremiah 31:3 (OT)

_____

_____

_____

_____

1 John 4:16 (NT)

_____

_____

_____

_____

9. God is just. He will judge and rule according to perfect fairness. Psalm 58:11 (OT)

_____

_____

_____

_____

10. God is faithful. He will never let you down and will always be true to His Word.

1 Thessalonians 5:24 (NT)

_____

_____

_____

_____

11. God is judge. Although He delights in goodness, His character is such that He must judge sin and immoral behavior. Leviticus 26:18 (OT)

_____

_____

_____

_____

John 3:36 (NT)

_____

_____

_____

_____

12. God is patient. Psalm 86:15 (OT)

_____

_____

_____

_____

13. God is judging and wrathful. Although He delights in goodness, His character is such that He must judge sin and immoral behavior. Leviticus 26:18 (OT)

_____
_____
_____
_____

John 3:36 (NT)

_____
_____
_____

14. God is patient. Psalm 86:15 (OT)

_____
_____
_____
_____

Lesson TWO

MAN IN HIS NATURAL STATE: A SINNER BEFORE GOD

This lesson and the next two will talk about man as a sinner. Man, as he naturally is, is a sinner. You might be wondering why these next three lessons are about sin. Be assured, the lessons on sin are not given first in order to depress you. Rather, they are covered first for the simple reason that no one can understand his need for God, unless he first sees himself as God sees him—as a sinner. Man is sinful and needs God. This is the teaching of the Bible. The next three lessons will show that all men are sinful.

Have you ever stopped to consider God's opinion of mankind? How does God describe mankind in the Bible? You are part of mankind, therefore these questions pertain to you. How does God describe you? This lesson will answer these questions and others. Please note the title of this chapter is *Man in His Natural State: A Sinner before God*. By *man in his natural state*, we mean the state of man outside of salvation. How does God view man before man comes to faith in Christ (or before man becomes a Christian, as the Bible defines Christian)? What does the Bible teach about man's relationship with God from the time he is born into the world?

I. BIBLE PROOF THAT ALL HUMAN BEINGS ARE SINNERS

The Bible very clearly teaches beyond dispute that all human beings are sinners. Look up each of the Scripture passages listed below and record only the portion of the verse plainly declaring that all people sin).

1. 1 Kings 8:46 (OT)

_____

_____

_____

_____

2. Psalm 14:2-3 (OT)

_____

_____

_____

_____

Please keep in mind that these two verses are talking of man as he naturally is—in other words, the condition he is in as soon as he is born into the world. The verses are speaking of man before he becomes a true Christian. Man is naturally corrupt, rotten, and evil in the sight of God. Man naturally does not seek God. He has turned aside from God and does no good. Before we move on, note that the verse says, *The Lord looks down from heaven on the sons of men.* This is how God sees man. Others might not view man in this way—and you might not ever see yourself in this way. All of us, to some degree, suffer self-deception as we view our sins. Many even claim that they have never sinned. But this is God's indictment. As He sits in heaven, He sees mankind in this way.

According to Psalm 14:2-3, how many have turned aside from seeking God? _____

Would this indictment include you? _____

How many do *good* according to verse 3? _____

It is important you understand that these verses are not talking of doing good to other people. No doubt, you often do good to your neighbors, friends, and relatives. When vs. 3 says, *there is none who doeth good*, it does not mean no one does good to other fellow humans. It means no one does good toward God. This is God's statement concerning natural man, or man before he becomes a Christian.

According to these verses, how many are corrupt? _____

In what ways do you see yourself as corrupt?

_____

_____

_____

_____

Perhaps it should be mentioned that sometimes when this passage of Scripture is comprehended, it causes anger, resentment, and denial.

3. Proverbs 20:9 (OT) This verse asks a rhetorical question. A rhetorical question is one asked merely for an effect, with no answer expected. Can anyone answer, that he or she is without sin? _____

4. Ecclesiastes 7:20 (OT)

_____

_____

_____

_____

Define *righteous*. (If you do not know the meaning, please take the time to look it up in the dictionary).

_____

_____

A universally accepted meaning of *righteous* is conformity to a standard. God has established a standard for man. Because God is perfect, He has established a perfect standard for man. God is without sin; therefore, He cannot accept sin in His presence. Because of His character, He expects sinlessness. This is all God can accept. For God to accept anything less would make His standards less than morally perfect.

According to Ecclesiastes 7:20, there is not a righteous man—there is not any man on earth who measures up to God's standard of perfection. (Do not let this 'bum' you out. If you understand this, you are on your way to finding God.) Since God's standard is perfection and God tells us in the Bible just what perfection is, what areas do you see in yourself as being imperfect? (If you want a good understanding of God's standard of perfection, take the time to read Matthew 5:21-7:27. Then state the areas you see where you do not measure up to His standard of perfection).

---

5. Romans 3:9 (NT)

Depending upon your knowledge of the Bible, you might or might not understand this verse. When the verse says, ...*both Jews and Gentiles, that they are all under sin,* it means the entire world or all of mankind. The Bible often divides man into two classes of people—Jews and Gentiles. The nation of Israel (Jews) were God's chosen people in the Old Testament—but even they were sinners.

Note, too, the verse says, *We have already made the charge that Jews and Gentiles alike are all under sin.* (This is what the author of Romans has been doing in chapters 1-3, proving the whole world is under the condemnation of sin. Take time to read these three chapters this week, keeping the purpose of the chapters in your mind). But for now, notice the word, *charge.* What does it mean to have charges pressed against an individual? If someone is *charged* with a crime, what does that mean?

_____

_____

_____

_____

To charge a person means to accuse a person. Here in Romans 3:9 Paul says, in effect, that we have already made the accusation that Jews and Gentiles alike are all under sin.

6. What does it mean to be under sin? If an alcoholic or a drug addict is under the influence, what does that mean?

_____

_____

_____

_____

7. Romans 3:23 (NT)

_____

_____

_____

_____

The Greek word for *have sinned*, means to miss the mark. The author of these lessons has hunted deer several times with a bow. In order to prepare for bow season, he has often shot target practice. More times than not, the arrow misses *the mark* or the bullseye. This is the idea of verse 23. All of mankind has strung his bow, drawn his arrow, and shot at God's bulls-eye of perfection. And all have missed the mark many times over! Men are sinners! Can you think of times that you have attempted to be perfect or do something perfectly and were not able?

_____

_____

_____

_____

8. Galatians 3:22 (NT)

_____

_____

_____

_____

What do you think of when you think of a prisoner? A person behind bars, locked up, chained, or controlled is the idea that goes through my mind. The whole world—you, me, everyone—is a prisoner chained, locked up, and controlled by sin. Take note, this verse says that *the Scripture hath concluded*. It matters not if I acknowledge I am not prisoner to sin or if you acknowledge you are. God's Word says we are. If we deny we are sinners, our argument is not with each other, but with God.

9. 1 John 1:10 (NT)

_____

_____

_____
_____

What do we make God out to be, if we dare to claim ourselves to be without sin?

_____
_____
_____
_____

How is it that, *His word has no place in our lives* if we claim to be without sin?

_____
_____
_____
_____

What does *His word* refer to?

_____
_____
_____
_____

From these nine passages, is there any doubt as to where man stands before God, his Creator? All men, without exception are sinners. This includes you—it includes me.

II. MAN'S CONSCIENCE TEACHES HIM HE IS A SINNER

We have just made the claim that every person is sinful. The source of authority used to make that claim is the Bible. This is the primary source to verify this truth. There is a secondary source that also making this same claim, our conscience. Based on the first lesson, this source would fall under the category of experience. We attribute

the Bible as the primary source, verifying the sinfulness of all men—
and look to the conscience as a secondary source. Let's analyze the
reasons for making this primary and secondary classification.

We have just seen that the Bible teaches that all men sin. The
Bible is inerrant (that is, it is without error) and infallible (that is, it
can never fail when it makes claims). But there is another indicator
that all men sin. It is each man's individual conscience. All men have
a conscience and each man's own conscience testifies to himself that
he sins. Before we look briefly at this in the Scriptures, you need to
understand a very important truth about your conscience.

The Bible is inerrant and infallible, but man's conscience is
neither inerrant nor infallible. In other words, man's conscience is not
a completely reliable source for indicating his sin. This is because,
as we have already learned, man is a sinner. Therefore, even his
conscience is marred by sin. It does not reveal his sin as accurately or
as completely as the Bible does. Nevertheless, man's conscience still
convinces him of sin.

1. Romans 2:12-15 (NT)—These verses might be a bit difficult
   to understand. Read and reread them. Pay special attention
   to verses 14-15. According to vs. 15, where has God written
   His law?

   _____

   _____

He has written His law on men's hearts, or on their inmost being. Man
has been created with God's requirements (this is what *law* means)
stamped into his heart. Because of this, men intuitively know God
has certain requirements for them.

This is why you can go to a remote tribe in Africa, where
people have never been exposed to the Bible, and see the similarities
regarding their code of ethics. They believe outright murder is wrong,

lying is wrong, stealing is wrong, etc. Even though they have never seen these things in the Bible, they believe these things because God has written his law on their hearts or conscience.

Every living person has felt guilt and this proves man's sinfulness. How does man's conscience bear witness to God's law? Man's thoughts either accuse him or defend him. Have you experienced guilt, because of wrongdoing? Can you see how this teaches you are sinful?

_____

_____

_____

_____

Maybe you have done some things wrong or committed sin no one else is aware of—not your parents, spouse, children, or anyone. Does your conscience eat at you? Does it secretly excuse you? This is because God has written His law in your heart. Your troubled conscience is proof you are a sinner. Keep in mind your conscience can deceive you, but the Bible will not.

I have a man (a good friend at that) who practically killed me one time on the basketball court. He shoved me into the wall, as I was making a lay-up. When I confronted him, his response was, "My conscience doesn't bother me. Therefore I don't think that I did anything wrong." Obviously, to me and to all who saw him shove me, his conscience failed him (assuming, of course, he was simply lying!) So, to some degree, a man's conscience proves his sinfulness. But the Bible is the only completely trustworthy statement as to man's natural condition before God—a sinner.

2. Romans 9:1 (NT) What does Paul claim his conscience confirms?

_____

_____

_____

Again, this proves a man's conscience acts as an inward judge as to his rightness or wrongness.

    3. 1 Timothy 4:1-2 (NT) This verse, definitely proves the conscience cannot be trusted as can the Bible. What does Paul say has happened to some men's consciences?

_____

_____

_____

_____

What do you think Paul meant by this?

_____

_____

_____

_____

Paul is saying these people had lost the sense of the wrongness of their actions. Their conscience had been so dulled by sin their conscience no longer worked accurately. Think of a habitual liar as an example. Perhaps at first his lies produced some guilt but after the habit formed, he then has the ability to lie without any guilt. Regarding this lying his conscience has been seared. The searing can take place in multiple ways within a person's conscience. There are many things people do, perhaps that you do, where you do not believe it is wrong and have no guilt over it, only to later realize that God deems it wrong in His Word. Again, this is the searing of the conscience. As you can see, conscience, unlike the Bible, is not an infallible indicator of man as a sinner. But to some extent, conscience does show each of us we are sinners.

Lesson THREE

MAN, AS A SINNER FROM BIRTH

Knowing now from Lesson Two that Scripture, God's Word, teaches that all men are sinners, have you ever wondered, "How could this be?" Why is it that sin is so universal, excluding no one? Doesn't it seem that someone, someplace, with over five billion people on the earth, would be sin-free? And yet Scripture plainly teaches that all people sin. Why? Does Scripture supply us with an answer? It sure does.

The Bible teaches all people sin because everyone is a descendant of Adam and Eve. Adam and Eve were the first couple in the human race. They disobeyed God in the Garden of Eden. (You can read their account in Genesis 2-3.) Their disobedience made them the first sinners. Since all of humanity are of Adam and Eve, we inherit their sinful nature at birth. Thus, we are born sinners. From the time we first have life, we are sinful. The following verses of Scripture prove this. (Again, for this lesson as you read each passage, list the portion teaching we are sinners from birth).

III. BIBLE PROOF THAT ALL ARE BORN SINNERS

4. Psalm 51:5 (OT) Read this verse carefully! When does a person become sinful?

_____

_____

57

David is the spokesman of Psalm 51. He says he was a sinner from birth. He even says he was a sinner, while he was forming in the womb—*sinful from the time my mother conceived me!* That is, from the time his father's sperm united with his mother's egg, he was a sinner. This means David (and mankind) was a sinner during the nine months he was forming in his mother's womb. One does not have to commit sin to become a sinner. While being knit together and molded in the womb, sin is part of man's very being. What an awesome thought!

This verse very clearly teaches an individual's sin is not due to one's environment. A bad environment may make it easier for sinners to express themselves, but a bad environment doesn't make one sin. Man forms as a sinner before he ever comes out of the womb. If society were clean and pure, men would still sin. They are born sinners.

A common question often asked at this point is: What happens to infants when they die? If infants are sinful, do they go to heaven or hell? This is a legitimate question, as we have just learned even infants are sinful. This is a question, however, not directly answered in the Bible. Nowhere is this issue addressed. A direct case cannot be dogmatically and Biblically made to support an infant going directly to heaven or directly to hell upon death. Because of that, we need to turn to the principles of Scripture.

One principle is that God is always good and He is always just. We do not have to worry about God not being fair. No matter what, we know His character is pure, sinless, righteous, and loving. We can commit these questions (such as infant death) into the hands of the loving and true God we know. We can simply trust Him and be assured He will do what is right. Some have attempted to reconcile this theological tension by saying babies that are baptized will go to heaven, because the baptism washes away original sin. Not only is this in direct opposition to the teachings of Scripture, it brings about a logical conclusion stating infants that are not baptized will go to hell. This is an obvious theological blunder. Simply trust God's character and love and commit these things to Him. (Deuteronomy 29:29)

> **5.** Job 14:1-4 (OT) According to vs 1, *man born of woman* is two things. What are the two things?

_____

_____

Notice the connection again between *man born of woman* and *full of trouble*. This verse again suggests man is sinful from birth. Look at vs 4. Can anyone bring what is pure from the impure? _____ Are all mothers impure (sinful)? Remember Chapter 2! Can impure mothers give birth to pure babies?

_____

> **6.** Job 15:14-16 (OT) According to vs. 16, what is man?

_____

> **7.** According to these verses, can God trust or depend on man to do what is right? _____

Additional proof that we are all born sinners is found in the principles of Genesis 1. There God set up a law of nature governing all reproduction. In Genesis 1:12, the land produced vegetation—plants bearing seed according to their kinds. And God saw that it was good. Notice the verse says the fruit tree yielded fruit according to its kind.

In other words, a cherry tree will produce cherries. This is a law of reproduction. It would be utterly impossible for a cherry tree to bear apples. It must bring forth fruit after its kind. This was also true in Genesis 1 regarding the creatures of the sea and of the land. Thus, this principle can be applied to man and his kind. When men reproduce, they will bring forth according to their kind. This is why Genesis 5:3 says that Adam had a son *in his own likeness, after his image*. Adam's son, Seth, was just like him, according to his kind. Adam was a sinner, thus Seth was born a sinner, his son was born a sinner, and so on, until it reaches you and me. How is it that there is not even one righteous person under heaven before God? Out of five billion plus, how is it that all are sinners?

_____

_____

_____

_____

We are all born sinners! My friend, perhaps your parents are the ideal parents. Perhaps, they have always taken care of you, provided for your need, and maybe you are even the beneficiary of their will. Maybe they have never done anything to hurt you! Well, know this for sure—when you were born, they passed along their sinful nature to you. This is why you sin. You are *according to their kind*. You might not sin to the extent of your parents, but you nevertheless do sin. Keep in mind, everyone you meet, whether fellow workers, friends, relatives, or neighbors, all are just like you and me. All are sinners, because they were born in that condition. You might be thinking, "It isn't fair I should be made a sinner because of Adam's sin. Why didn't God create each individual to obey or disobey God for himself? I really have no say in the fact that I am a sinner, since it is automatically passed along."

As already said, this is the law of reproduction. The plant, and animal, and human kind reproduce *according to their kind*. This principle was established before Adam ever disobeyed God and thus became a sinner. Suppose Adam had obeyed God, what would have happened then? All of Adam's descendants would have been holy, righteous, pure, and innocent. The laws of reproduction would still have governed Adam's offspring. Adam would have been holy, thus his offspring would have been *according to his kind.* Had this been the case and Adam had retained his innocence, all of us would now be innocent—and no one would question God for this or think it to be unfair!

The Scriptures declare to us that God is the Greater Creator and we are the creation. We are not the ones who judge what is fair and what is not fair. It is part of our rebellious sinful nature to scream foul at the issue of being born sinners. God's will is always what prevails and we can rest assured that He is fair in all circumstances, as He defines fairness.

As you'll learn later—be patient—as Adam represented mankind, thus all were made sinners. Even so, Jesus Christ represented sinners and those coming to Him in faith will be forgiven.

IV. BIBLE PROOF THAT ALL MEN HAVE A SINFUL NATURE

Man's physical birth into sin, having come from sinful parents, gives man a sinful nature. *By sinful nature* means that since man was born a sinner, he has inherited his parents' sinful character, disposition, natural instincts, desires, and appetites. Another way of saying this is, it is man's bent in life to sin. Man is not inherently good, but inherently evil. Man enjoys and pursues evil. Let us look at several passages of Scripture proving man's tendency is toward sin. Copy the portion of each verse that proves this assertion.

Genesis 6:5-6 (OT) What portion of this verse indicates man's natural tendency is toward sin?

_____

_____

In the Bible, the word *heart* has various meanings. It can mean a) the mind—where man thinks, b) the emotions, c) the will, or d) the physical heart muscle. Which of these is the obvious meaning of the word *heart* in Genesis 6:5?

_____
_____
_____
_____

Man's mind is, therefore, focused upon what?

_____

Job 15:14-16 (OT) How readily and easily does man pursue sin according to the last phrase of verse 16?

_____
_____

Do you enjoy water, milk, or pop to drink with a nice meal? Of course, you do. We all drink some beverage every day. God's Word in Job 15:16 compares our love for sin to our love for water. Our birth into sin made us this way. We have a natural love, desire, instinct, and inclination for sin.

1. Job 20:12a (OT) says, *though evil is sweet in his mouth...* How does this statement indicate man's appetite for sin?

_____
_____
_____
_____

2. Proverbs 2:12-14 (OT) What do sinners delight in? What do sinners rejoice in?

_____

Those were some of the OT passages proving man's tendency is toward sin. It is his nature to sin. Let's now look at some NT passages proving this.

3. Romans 3:11-12 (NT) What phrases in these verses prove man's nature is contrary to God?

Vs 11

_____
_____
_____
_____

Vs 12

_____
_____
_____
_____

4. Romans 3:15-16 (NT) Read this. Please note it says that men's feet are swift to shed blood. Swift means *quick or without hesitation.* We all hurt other people. That's because it is our nature to. Also, ruin and misery are marks of our conduct, according to vs 16. Why? Because our nature or natural tendency and inclination is towards unholy, ungodly things.

5. Read Romans 1:18-32 (NT) Based on the entire passage, comment on the significance or reason behind the truth of verse 32.

_____

My friend, everyone (including you and me) are bent toward sin. We have a natural taste for sin. We inherited it from our parents, who in turn inherited it from their parents, so forth and so forth, until we reach the first parents of mankind, Adam and Eve.

- Is man inherently good? Are you inherently good?

_____

- Is the one who is leading you through this study inherently good?

_____

- Do you now understand how you became a sinner? How?

_____
_____
_____
_____

- What did you give your children at their conception?

_____

- Therefore, are they sinners as well?

_____

V. NATURAL MAN'S RELATIONSHIP TO ORIGINAL SIN

Did Adam's sin only affect me because it gave me my sinful nature? I wish it only affected me that way, but that just isn't so. The Scriptures teach that not only did Adam's sinful act of disobedience give me my sinful nature, but also Adam's sin made me guilty before the Holy God. In other words, I am held accountable for Adam's sin. Let's look at passages of Scripture proving this.

6. Romans 5:12 (NT) What entered the world through one man?

_____

7. Who is the *one man* being spoken of here? (see vs 14, if needed) _____

8. What entered the world *through one man's sin*, according to vs 12? _____

Notice closely the verse goes on to say, *and in this way* or either through Adam's sin, *death came to all men.* The teaching of this verse is this: Through one man, Adam, sin entered the world. And by his sin, death entered the world and *came to all men.* The term *death* in this verse includes all types of death, but it refers primarily to spiritual death. In Genesis 2:17, you find God told Adam immediately following creation that, *in the day that you* (Adam) *eat of the tree of knowledge of good and evil, you will die.* Adam did die spiritually.

There are three types of death spoken of in the Scripture.

Spiritual Death—This is man in his total being, separated from God, or as Ephesians 4:18 states, *alienated from the life of God.*

Physical Death—This is when the soul separates from the body. This is what has occurred every time we attend a funeral.

Eternal Death—In Scripture this is called the second death (Revelation 20:14). Man, following judgment, is cast into the lake of fire to burn forever.

9. Please take the time to explain in your own words with what each of these three deaths mean and when each of them takes place. (I have experienced many people who have not had a clear understanding of these three deaths.)

_____

_____

_____

_____

10. When does spiritual death take place?

_____

Physical death and eternal death are the results of spiritual death. Adam died spiritually by that one sin. The verse then says spiritual death passed upon all men. It is interesting, most people think people are born spiritually alive with a relationship with God—and when they lead a life of sin as an adult, they spiritually die. This could not be further from the Bible's teaching. People are born spiritually dead with a broken relationship with God. If they remain in this spiritually dead state up to the point of physical death, they will undergo eternal death. What every person needs is to go from spiritual death to spiritual birth. This is why Jesus says in John 3, that unless a person is born again (this time spiritually, not just physically) he will not enter into the kingdom of heaven. This need of spiritual birth is what this entire study is about.

11. Copy John 3:3

_____

_____

_____

_____

This is where the phrase *born again* comes from. It comes directly from the mouth of Jesus. The bottom line is you do not do something to become spiritually dead, you already are dead. What you need is to do something to be made spiritually alive. These lessons are intended to show you exactly what that means. But for now, let's continue to understand our sinful nature even more.

12. Romans 5:18 (NT) says that *the result of one trespass was condemnation for all men*. What did Adam's one sin do for all men?

_____

What does condemnation mean? It means a declaration of guilt. To condemn a man is to declare him to be unrighteous or to not measure up to the set standard.

13. Romans 3:23 (NT) Thus there are at least three things Adam's sin did to you and me:

a) It gave us our sinful nature.

b) It made us guilty before God.

c) It made us spiritually dead.

Serious, indeed, are the effects of that one act of disobedience. We are all held accountable for Adam's sin— what Bible scholars call *original sin*. It is called this because it was the first sin. However, original sin is not the only sin of which all are guilty. We are also guilty of many actual sins. It is the topic of actual sins we will take up in the next lesson. This principle of *one representing all* is not uncommon in the Scriptures, nor in human experience. In the Old Testament, the High Priest represented the entire nation of Israel before God. In fact, if the priest sinned, guilt came upon the whole nation (see Leviticus 4:1-3). Often, in the Old Testament, one man's sin brought judgment upon all. Consider for example, Adam's sin in Joshua 6-7. Consider also, Exodus 20:4-6. There God promises to punish *the children for the sin of the fathers.* How often in human experience today are children punished due to an alcoholic or lazy father? Children reap the ill effects of their parents. Sin is universal.

Before going through this study, you may have thought sinners were just the **really bad people** of this world. You may not have even considered yourself as inherently sinful. As everyone else, you were born sinful with a broken relationship with God. This is so crucial to understand, because no one can fix something if they do not know it has been broken. May God continue to reveal these deep and important truths to you from His Word.

Do you have any questions about the first three lessons? If so, please list them, so you can discuss them with a Christian friend or a pastor.

Lesson FOUR

DEFINING ACTUAL SIN AND UNDERSTANDING THE CONSEQUENCES OF SIN

Thus far we have learned that all men are born as sinners. We are born this way because two impure parents (sinners themselves) can only give birth to impure children. We also have learned our birth into sin gave us our sinful nature—that is, our inherent sinful character, disposition, natural instincts, desires, love and appetites for sin. The sin of Adam that caused all these problems in our life is the sin known as the *original sin*. In this lesson we wish to discuss *actual sin*. Actual sin means the sins you and I personally commit in our lifetime. Original sin is the sin of Adam that adversely affected you and me. Actual sin is our own sin resulting from our sinful nature, which we received from Adam's original sin. In this lesson, we will answer two questions, in regard to actual sin.

1) Why are actual sins committed?

_____

2) What are actual sins?

_____

I. WHY ARE ACTUAL SINS COMMITTED?

Several texts of Scripture make it clear that man's everyday sins are the result of a sinful nature. Let's look at a few of those texts.

1. Luke 6:43-45 (NT) Read these verses carefully first. It is important you know that Jesus is comparing human nature to a tree in these verses. In verses 43-44, Jesus talks about two different types of trees, a good tree and a bad tree. Then in verse 45, Jesus begins talking about nature.

According to verse 43, can a bad tree bring forth good fruit? According to verse 45, can an evil man bring forth good fruit? Based upon our lessons up to this point are men good or bad trees? Can bad men then produce good things?

_____

Notice Jesus continues by saying, *for of the abundance of the, heart his mouth speaketh.* In other words, that which is within man, his heart, comes out through the mouth. What is man's heart or internal being? Is it good or bad?

_____

2. Look now at Jeremiah 17:9 (OT). What is man's heart?

_____

According to Luke 6:45, what results from a bad heart?

_____
_____
_____
_____

The teaching of Luke 6:43-45 is clearly this. Good men bring forth good things. Bad men bring forth bad things. But since man is evil, his nature is such that he can only bring forth evil things. Our sinful nature is what causes our sinful words, thoughts, and deeds.

3. Mark 7:21-23 (NT) Where does Jesus say that evil thoughts, sexual immorality, theft, murder, and so on, come from?

_____

How can this be? It is because man has a sinful nature. His sinful nature gives rise to his actual sins.

II. WHAT ARE ACTUAL SINS?

Now that you know why actual sin is committed, let me attempt to define what actual sin is. Actual sin is committed by all of us in so many ways. It is very difficult to be brief in our definition. We all speak about what is sinful, but can sin be defined in a coherent way? I believe the Apostle John in 1 John 3:4 (NT) summed up all that constitutes actual sin. Turn there please.

1 John 3:4 (NT) What is John's brief definition of actual sin?

_____
_____
_____
_____

Do you know the meaning of this verse? What is lawlessness?

_____
_____
_____
_____

Lawlessness consists of acts going beyond or falling short of the limits prescribed by the law. Thus, when the Apostle John says, "Sin is lawlessness," he means that when you and I sin, we go beyond the limits of God's law or fall short of God's law. Simplified, this means we commit actual sin, when anything we do does not conform entirely to the boundaries of God's law. Notice what J.C. Ryle said in defining sin: _I say, furthermore, that sin, 'to speak more particularly,_ *consists in doing, saying, thinking, or imagining anything that is not in perfect conformity with the mind and law of God. 'Sin' in short, as the Scripture saith, is 'the transgression of the law,' 1 John 3:4. The slightest outward or inward departure from absolute mathematical parallelism with God's revealed will and character constitutes a sin, and at once makes us guilty in God's sight.*

Note please, Ryle says: *a sin ... consists in doing, saying, thinking, or imagining anything that is not in perfect conformity with the mind and law of God.* Scripture teaches, as Ryle indicates, actual sin is committed in at least three ways: 1) Thinking or Thought; 2) Saying or Word; 3) Doing or Deed. Let's look at some Scriptures teaching this.

A. Thought

In each of the verses given below, list only the portion teaching that men sin in thought.

Mark 7:21 (NT)

_____

_____

_____

_____

Proverbs 15:26 (OT)

_____

_____

_____

_____

Jeremiah 4:14 (OT)

_____

_____

73

_____

_____

Genesis 6:5 (OT)

_____

_____

_____

_____

We could go to many other verses to prove we commit sin through our thoughts. However, these are sufficient to convict any honest individual. Anytime you think an evil thought, a lustful thought, a bitter thought, a foolish thought, or any thought running contrary to God's mind and law, you have committed an actual sin.

Have you ever had someone treat you meanly—someone who really did you wrong? How did you respond? Probably you had many vengeful thoughts race through your mind toward that individual. This is normal and to be expected—remember, it is your nature to be this way! However, these vengeful thoughts were, and are, sin.

Romans 2:16 (NT) Copy this verse:

_____

_____

_____

_____

The verse teaches God will judge the secrets of men at the great Judgment Day. What is more secret than your thoughts? Only you and God know the thoughts that lie in the deep recesses of your mind. At Judgment Day, God will judge them!

74

B. Word

Matthew 12:36-37 (NT)

_____

_____

_____

_____

_____

_____

Notice the verses say that we will give an account on Judgment Day of every careless word. It will be our words that acquit us or condemn us. Why will we give account of every idle word and why will our words either acquit or condemn us? Simply because we all sin.

Romans 3:11-14 (NT)

_____

_____

_____

_____

Verses 11-12 tell us that no one, including you and me, is righteous or good. Verses 13-14 then tells us one way that we are not good. It says we are not good because of our throat, tongues, lips, and mouth—our speech organs. Our tongues use deceit, poison is within our lips, and cursing and bitterness proceed from our mouths. Do you see the teaching of this passage? It is very clear. We sin through our spoken words, our oral speech.

Ephesians 4:29 (NT)

_____

_____

_____

A command is given. We are to allow no unwholesome talk to proceed from our mouth. Why? Unwholesome speech is sin.

James 3:3-10 (NT) What is the point of these verses?

_____

_____

_____

_____

C. Deed

Mark 7:21-23 (NT) What sins, according to these verses, do we commit through deed?

_____

_____

_____

_____

1 Thessalonians 4:3-5 (NT) What is God's view of physical intimacy outside the bounds of marriage?

_____

_____

_____

_____

Hebrews 13:4 (NT) What does God say He will do to those that violate this standard?

_____

_____

_____

The issue of sexual relations outside of marriage has always been clear in the Scriptures. It is condemned by God. Sexual fulfillment is intended to be manifested in the confines of marriage. This is the way God created it. Our society, particularly in recent days, has drastically departed from this clear Biblical standard. The moral standard has dropped so low that you are commended if you only have sexual relations in a serious and committed relationship.

Men and women who are not married live together today without any guilt. Couples living together out of wedlock is accepted today in our society. People are even beginning to claim that God does not look down on sex outside of marriage, as long as precautions are taken and there is a serious commitment between the two parties. This is perfectly acceptable in relativistic society (remember Chapter 1). But this is a clear departure from the absolute standards of the Bible and the clear will of God. God is the author of these physical desires. They are good and He intended them for pleasure—but He clearly intended them to be fulfilled in the institution that He established called *marriage*. Do you see from the Scriptures that sexual relations (or any sexual contact—as well as boyfriend and girlfriend living together) outside the bounds of marriage is sinful and not honoring to God?

Galatians 5:19-21 (NT) List all of the sins named in these verses.

_____

_____

_____

_____

Have you committed any of these? Which ones? Maybe you never committed the sin of murder or rape, etc.—but what about idolatry? Have you ever found your supreme pleasure and joy in anything other than God? Then you've committed the actual sin of idolatry. What about hatred? This is a sin no one would ever deny committing. What about covetousness? Have you ever secretly desired your neighbor's house, car, boat, or clothing? If so, then you've coveted! God says this is sin. Thus, we see there are sins of thought, word, and deed.

Before we end this section, let me acquaint you with our sins in a deeper way. Scripture teaches there are sins of commission and sins of omission. Sins of commission are active sins we commit by doing the things we ought not to do. Sins of omission are sins we commit by leaving undone the things we ought to do.

Please explain in your own words the difference between sins of commission and sins of omission:

_____
_____
_____
_____

We already looked at sins of commission, when we looked at Mark 7 and Galatians 5. Let us now look at a verse speaking of the sin of omission (leaving undone the things we ought to do).

James 4:17 (NT)

_____
_____
_____
_____

Name some sins you are aware of that would be sins of omission for you.

_____
_____
_____
_____

In other words, when we know to do good, but we don't do it, it is sin. Pray, obey God, worship God, love our neighbor, obey our government, these are good words and if not done, we've committed sin. One man said, "Take heed of sins of omission. It is a sin to omit any good which is commanded, as well as to commit any evil

78

which is forbidden—not to do what we ought, as well as to do what we ought not." Have you ever left any good thing undone through procrastination, laziness, or stubbornness? If so, you've sinned. One man prayed on his deathbed, "Lord, forgive me all my sins, and especially my sins of omission." (Ryle).

Realizing we sin through thought, word, and deed, which of these ways is the most secretive to others?

_____

Is any one of the three more secluded from God than the other two?

_____

Which do we attempt to seclude the most?

_____

I can hear your words, you can hear mine. I can see your deeds, you can see mine. But even right now, I have no idea what you are thinking, and vice versa! But God knows!

III. THE CONSEQUENCES OF OUR SIN

This lesson considers the results of sin or the wages of sin. Specifically, we will answer the questions, What penalty has God attached to man and his sin? What has God decreed to do unto man because of his sin?

Genesis 2:15-17(OT) God placed one prohibition upon the first man, Adam. What was it?

_____

_____

_____

_____

What penalty did God attach to the prohibition? In other words, if man broke God's command in verse 17, what did God promise the consequence to be?

_____

God promised Adam in Genesis 2:17 that if he ate of the forbidden tree, he would surely die. Did Adam die? He most certainly did. If you need to refresh your memory concerning the meaning of death in the Bible, look back at Lesson 3. It is important you see within the early pages of Genesis that the penalty attached to sin is death.

1. Ezekiel 18:4 (OT) In this text, who does God claim to own?

_____

What penalty is here attached to sin?

_____

2. Romans 6:23 (NT) What are the wages of sin?

_____

3. Romans 8:13 (NT) What is affirmed as sure to happen to all who live according to their sinful nature?

_____

Do you think Paul means physical, spiritual, or eternal death? (Look back at Lesson 3 for the distinction of each.)

_____

Paul obviously doesn't mean physical death, because even Christians (people who no longer live by their sinful nature) physically die. So, Paul doesn't mean that type of death. Neither does he mean spiritual death, because all who are living by their sinful nature are spiritually dead. Paul here says, in the future tense, that if you live according to the sinful nature, you will die. The death spoken of here is a future punishment, eternal death in the lake of fire. Sin results in that!

4. Romans 2:8 (NT) What is promised in this verse to those who follow evil?

_____

The Bible teaches that God has attached the penalty of death to man's sin. This is the consequence of being a sinner. The death promised is eternal death. Eternal death is separation from God forever in the Lake of Fire, following physical death. This threat hangs over the head of every sinner. Therefore, does it hang over your head? _____

I am fully aware this is not a popular topic to mention. However, it is a Bible truth. It should strike terror into man's heart!

5. Revelation 20:11-15 (NT) What is the teaching of these verses in your own words?

_____

_____

_____

_____

According to verse 12, who stands before the throne?

_____

What are the books used for, according to verse 12?

_____

According to verse 13, what is this judgment based upon?

_____

According to verse 14, what is the Lake of Fire called?

_____

The second death is eternal death. Physical death is the first death. As mentioned in Lesson Three, death is never extinction or cessation of being. Death means separation or departure. To be cast into the Lake of Fire, the second death, is to be separated from God forever and ever in fire. According to vs 15, is anyone thrown into the Lake of Fire? _____

In conjunction with the above verses, look at Revelation 21:8 (NT). Who will be in the Lake of Fire?

_____

6. 2 Thessalonians 1:8-9 (NT) According to these two verses, what will happen to those who do not know God or obey the Gospel?

_____

7. Meditate on the above passage of Scripture. Have you ever considered the depth of God's judgment and wrath?

_____

Remember Lesson One, many people think of God only as love and have never thought about God's judgment, wrath, and eternal punishment. Make no mistake, God judges all sin.

How long will their destruction be according to verse 9?

_____

Remember death never means extinction. It always means separation or departure. According to 2 Thessalonians 1:8-9, man will be shut out of God's presence and it will it be everlasting.

8. Matthew 7:21-23 (NT) According to verse 23, what will Jesus say to evil doers on Judgment Day?

_____

Away from me implies separation or departure. The Scriptures teach God has attached the penalty of death to sin. While the penalty of death includes physical and spiritual death, ultimately these two will result in eternal death. Eternal death is death in hell. Death means separation from God in hell forever. This is the penalty attached to sin.

There is no chance for recovery once in hell. It will be millenniums of torment.

Please take time on your own to read Matthew 10:28 (NT) and Luke 16:19-31 (NT). These two texts describe the horrors of hell. Do you understand what lies in your future as the penalty for your sin?

_____

Do you fear hell?

_____

Following the next lesson, we will look at the hope, the only hope, offered by God for man's deliverance from hell. Jesus Christ is the answer.

Lesson FIVE

JESUS CHRIST, GOD IN HUMAN FLESH

You have just completed the first part of this booklet, consisting of lessons on sin. Perhaps for the first time in your life, you see yourself as you truly are. God says you are a sinner. You have a sinful nature, inherited from your folks. It is very natural for you to sin. Sin comes easily for you. But, you're not alone! Sin comes easy for all people. At least until they become Christians!

In the next part of the book, we are going to examine the Bible to see what God has done to handle man's sin problem. Though mankind is in a terrible predicament, God has not deserted us and left us in despair. God has provided a remedy for the sins of the world. That remedy is JESUS CHRIST!

In today's lesson, our objective is this—we will take the Holy Scriptures and prove Jesus Christ was God in human flesh. This is called the Divine Incarnation—God manifested Himself in human flesh. Let's begin by looking at passages of Scripture where Jesus is called God.

I. SCRIPTURES IDENTIFYING JESUS CHRIST AS GOD

Isaiah 7:14 (OT) Immanuel means *God with us*. What do you think Isaiah means by this?

_____

_____

_____

_____

This verse was written over 700 years before Jesus Christ was born by the virgin Mary. Note that it says that a virgin will be with child and will give birth to a son. This verse then is an OT prophecy (an OT statement of what would come to pass in the future). Did all of this come to pass as predicted here? Well, let's see.

Matthew 1:18-23 (NT) Note verse 18 specifically. What does the phrase *before they came together* mean?

_____

_____

_____

_____

Was Mary a virgin then, as was foretold over 700 years earlier in Isaiah 7:14? _____

Look at vs 21. What gender would her child be? Male or Female? Now notice verse 22. Who does the word *prophet* refer to?

_____

Now finally look at vs 23. What was Jesus called?

_____

What does this title say about Jesus?

_____

Who was Jesus Christ, then? He was God in human flesh. It was foretold in Isaiah 7:14, over 700 years before Christ was born of a virgin. It was foretold in complete detail. Matthew 1:18-23 records the fulfillment of that prophecy.

John 1:1 (NT) Who does the "Word" refer to in this verse?

_____

Complete the sentence: *In the beginning was the Word, and the Word was with God and the Word was*

_____

_____

_____

_____

Now look at verse 14. According to this verse, what did *the Word* become? _____

Who then was *the Word* that became flesh?

_____

Became flesh in verse 14 means that God, or the Word, became human. Jesus Christ was God Incarnate (Jesus Christ was God in human flesh). Amazing indeed, but true!

In 2 Peter 1:1 (NT) Jesus Christ is given two names. What are they?

_____

_____

_____

_____

II. JESUS POSSESSED ABILITIES ONLY GOD POSSESSES

He claimed the ability to forgive sins.

1. Mark 2:1-12 (NT) Read this passage. Jesus did something that only God can do. He healed a cripple and forgave his sins. Note in verse 7 that Jesus' opponents accused Him of blasphemy (to speak mockingly of God). They believed He was mocking God, because He forgave the cripple's sins. They knew that only God could forgive sins. So, when Jesus said to the cripple in verse

5, *Son, thy sins be forgiven thee*, they interpreted Jesus to mean I am God. I can forgive sins. In their eyes this was blasphemy. They thought Jesus was mocking God, because He was claiming to be God.

2. Jesus forgave this man of all his sins, even the sins done to other people. Jesus was making a direct claim of Deity (God) and was interpreted as such by His opponents. In the OT, before Christ was born of the virgin Mary, power to forgive sins was ascribed to God alone. Now Jesus appears on the scene, claiming He can forgive sins. Thus, Jesus is claiming to be God.

III. JESUS ACCEPTED WORSHIP FROM MEN AND WOMEN

When Jesus walked upon the earth, he was repeatedly worshipped. This is significant, because only God is to be worshipped. If Jesus was not God in human flesh, then He should not have accepted the worship of others! But, He not only accepted worship from others, He even encouraged it!

1. Matthew 14:33 (NT) Does Jesus accept their worship?

_____

If He wasn't God, then He would have had an obligation to stop their worship by saying something like, "No, no you've got it all wrong. Don't worship me, I'm only a man." But Jesus always accepts worship. Compare it to Acts 14:8-18 where many people wanted to worship the Apostle Paul. Paul stopped them in verse 15 by saying, *Sirs, why do ye these things? We also are men of like passions with you...*? If Jesus was only a man, even if He was a great man, He would have had no right to accept worship from other men. But He accepted worship from others, because He was God in human flesh.

2. John 20:24-28 (NT) What does Thomas call Jesus in verse 28?

_____

3. Does Christ stop him and say, "No, no, Thomas! You're all wrong. I'm not God." _____

Wouldn't you expect Jesus to correct Thomas, if Jesus wasn't truly God? _____

Jesus was either God and thus accepted the praise heaped upon Him from Thomas, because it was the proper thing to do—or Jesus was a deceiver who accepted the title *God* from Thomas, when in fact, He wasn't God. **No, Jesus was God!**

The following verses also illustrate times when Jesus was worshipped and never once did forbid their worship. Why? Because He was God. Matthew 28:9; 28:17; Luke 24:52; John 9:39.

IV. JESUS IS CALLED THE CREATOR OF ALL THINGS

1. Genesis 1:1 (OT) According to this verse, who created all things? _____

2. John 1:1-3, 14 (NT) According to these four verses, who created all things?

_____

_____

Do you see the connection with Genesis 1:1?

_____

In Genesis 1:1, God is said to have created all things. In John 1:1-3, Jesus is said to have created all things. Who was Jesus then?

_____

V. JESUS CLAIMED TO BE GOD—EVEN HIS OPPONENTS SAID HE MADE SUCH CLAIMS

1. John 10:30-33 (NT) What is the claim of Jesus in verse 30?

_____

2. His claim is that He (Jesus) is equal to the Father. What do the Jews understand Jesus to mean according to verse 33?

_____

The reaction of the Jews to Jesus' statement, *I and the Father are One*, was to stone Him. They reacted this way because Jewish law demanded capital punishment for anyone falsely claiming to be God. Doesn't it seem, had Jesus not been God, that He would have said, "Hold the stones, Men. I've been misinterpreted?" But Jesus could not say that, because He had been interpreted properly. His opponents correctly understood that Jesus claimed to be God.

3. Matthew 21:14-16 (NT) What are the miracles Jesus performed in verse 14?

_____

According to verse 15, what is the response of the children to these healings? *Hosanna to the Son of David* means *praise to the Son of David*. The children who witnessed the miracles of Jesus, dealing with the blind and the lame, began to praise Jesus.

Note the reaction of the chief priests and the teachers of the law (the religious leaders) to the miracles and the worship of these children to Jesus. They were indignant, meaning they were angry. You would expect the chief priest and teachers of the law mentioned in verse 15 to be impressed. They have just seen miracles before their own eyes and they have seen children praising Jesus. But they were not impressed. To the contrary, verse 15 informs us of their anger.

Why were they indignant? It wasn't because of the healing of the blind and the lame. Rather, it was because the children were crying out, "Hosanna to the Son of David." They were offering praise and worship to Jesus. The children were worshipping Jesus. The chief priest and teachers of the law wanted Jesus to stop the children's worship of Him. They said in verse 16, *Hearest thou what these say?* In other words, the children are blaspheming by worshipping You. God alone is to be worshipped. Don't you hear them? Shut them up.

But note carefully Jesus' response in verse 16b. *Yea; have ye never read, Out of the mouth of babes and sucklings thou hast perfected praise?* This is a quote from Psalm 8:2, which declares that God ordained or prepared children to praise Him. So, Jesus defends the praise offered to Himself. On the basis of Psalm 8:2, God had prepared praise for Himself. Jesus is thus equating Himself with God.

4. John 5:16-18 (NT) In these verses, the Jews were angry with Jesus and desired to kill Him for two reasons. What were the two reasons?

_____

_____

_____

_____

According to verse 18, did the Jews believe Jesus was making a claim to Deity (to being God)?

_____

Did Jesus correct their understanding?

_____

Were they misunderstanding Jesus, or was Jesus claiming to be God?

_____

My friend, Jesus Christ truly did stand head and shoulders above all others who have ever lived. He was God, clad in human flesh.

This is why so many people worship Jesus Christ. They understood He claimed to be God, with all of the evidence. His perfect life, His miracles, His wisdom, and His exhaustive knowledge support His claim. Jesus Christ was completely and totally sinless. He never sinned in thought, word, or deed. He is the only perfect human who ever lived.

In John 8:46 Jesus offered a challenge only a perfect being would dare make. He looked his opponents in the eye and said, "Can any of you prove me guilty of sin?" If Jesus had possessed any character blemishes, you can bet His opponents would have seized the opportunity to point out His sins. Jesus was not afraid to be thoroughly examined, even by His opponents. He knew He was sinless. On the other hand, all impostors who have appeared, falsely claiming to be God, have had serious character flaws. Their claim was not taken seriously by very many people, because their blemishes were so apparent. Literally thousands, however, have taken Jesus' claim of being God seriously. This is because Jesus had no sin. His conduct and character supported His claim.

5. Exodus 3:11 (OT) Here God the Father is speaking with Moses. God calls Moses to lead the Israelites and they might question him. Moses asks God in verse 13 what name he should refer to when they ask what God's name is. In verse 14, what does God say in answer to Moses' question?

_____

6. John 8:54-59 (NT) In this passage Jesus is interacting with the Pharisees. They were the legalists of His day. They were accusing Jesus of doing His miracles through the power of demons. Jesus told them, *Abraham* (who the Pharisees looked up to as their father) *rejoiced to see my day*. What is the Pharisee's response in verse 57?

_____

_____

_____

_____

What title did Jesus use regarding Himself at the end of verse 58? _____

Obviously, Jesus was referencing Himself as equal to the Father. The title I AM was used only by God Almighty, the creator of the universe. After looking at verse 59, do you think the Pharisees knew Jesus was making Himself equal with God? Why?

_____

_____

_____

_____

This connection between Exodus 3 and John 8 is an excellent proof of Jesus' own claim of being God. There is perhaps no greater passage making this clearer. There is no question Jesus claimed to be God in human flesh. It is amazing indeed that the Great I AM, the God of the universe, was walking this earth interacting with men and women.

7. Isaiah 44:6-8 (OT) compared with Revelation 22:12-16 (NT). Who is the spokesperson in verse 6?

_____

What does God call Himself in the middle of verse 6?

_____

According to vs 6, is there any other God besides the God of this verse? _____

God says that there is no other God but Him and He calls Himself, *the First and the Last*. Now compare the following verse. Read Revelation 22:12-16 (NT).

What does Jesus call Himself in verse 13?

_____

What is the connection with Isaiah 44:6?

_____

In Isaiah 44:6, God called Himself "the First and the Last."

In Revelation 22:13, Jesus called Himself, "the First and the Last."

How can this be? It is so, because Jesus Christ was and is God.

8. Look also at Revelation 1:8. How does God describe Himself?

_____

Look at Revelation 22:13. How does Jesus describe Himself?

_____

Again, do you see the connection? In Revelation 1:8 the Lord God says, _I am the Alpha and Omega._ In Revelation 22:13, Jesus says, _I am the Alpha and Omega._ How can Jesus claim the title God claims in Revelation 1:8? He can make such a claim, because Jesus is God.

9. Before going through this lesson, did you realize Jesus was not God's creation, but literally God in the flesh? Because sin separates us from God, and because every human sacrifice would be a sinful sacrifice, no dependent of Adam could pay for the sins of the world. God the Father sent God the Son to become human (or become flesh) to be that one and only sacrifice. God had to do what man could not do on His own. This is why understanding Jesus was God in human flesh is essential. If He wasn't God, then He would be sinful— and if He was sinful, He could not pay for our sins.

When we worship Jesus Christ, we are not worshipping a mere man, we are worshipping the God-man. Jesus was fully God and fully man. If you take away Jesus' deity, you take away Jesus Christ.

<u>Jesus is God!</u>

Lesson SIX

THE PURPOSE OF GOD BECOMING MAN (INCARNATION)

Jesus Christ was God in human flesh! That truth is known as the incarnation. Have you ever considered the purpose behind the incarnation? Why did Jesus Christ leave the glories of heaven to assume an earthly existence? This question will be answered in this lesson. God has several purposes in His Son becoming man. The various reasons for the incarnation will be learned in this lesson. Simply stated, Jesus Christ became man, in order to restore sinners to God.

Through the fall of Adam, man's relationship with God was broken. Since all of mankind are descendants of the original sinful pair (Adam and Eve), all are born sinful and are thus alienated from God and under His wrath (Romans 2:8-9). Jesus Christ came as the Second Adam (1 Corinthians 15:45) to undo the work of the First Adam. Christ came into the world to redeem sinners (1 Timothy 1:15).

I. JESUS CHRIST BECAME MAN, IN ORDER TO DIE ON THE CROSS FOR SINNERS, PAY FOR THEIR SINS IN FULL, AND RESTORE THEM TO GOD'S LOVING FAVOR

96

Why did God become man? Let's allow the Scriptures to speak for themselves. (In each of the passages listed below, copy the portion of the verse that speaks of why God came to this earth.)

1. 1 Timothy 1:15 (NT)

_____

2. Luke 5:29-32 (NT)

_____

3. Matthew 1:21 (NT)

_____

From these three verses, you should be able to clearly see why God (Christ) became man. He came to this earth to save sinful people from their sins. And who are the sinful people? You and me, as our previous lessons discussed. We are the sinners. Even His name, Jesus, had this meaning—He would save His people from their sins. Look at some other verses.

4. Titus 2:11-14 (NT)

_____

_____

_____

_____

Did He ever succumb to temptation?

_____

5. Hebrews 7:26 (NT)

_____

_____

_____

_____

6. John 8:46 (NT) Would you ever dare, as your enemies, or even friends, do this? Why not?

_____

_____

_____

_____

The above five passages are sufficient to prove Jesus' sinlessness. However, in case you desire to pursue this further, there are many more Bible verses which fortify this important truth. Here are a few of them: 1 John 3:3; Hebrews 9:14; 1 Peter 1:19; 1 John 1:5; and John 14:30. The above emphasis is important for this reason: If Jesus Christ was guilty of sin Himself, then He would need to be punished for His own sin. As we saw in Chapter Five, *the wages of sin is death.* Since Jesus was sinless, having no sin of His own, He didn't fall under God's condemnation of death. Being sinless, He had no sin of His own for which to be punished. You might wonder then, "Why did He die on the cross?" and "Why did He say to the Father when hanging on the cross, 'My God, my God, why hast thou forsaken me?'" (Mark 15:34). The answer to those questions is that Jesus' death was vicarious (in the place of others).

II. THE VICARIOUS DEATH OF JESUS (ON BEHALF OF OTHERS)

Since Jesus' death was not punishment for His own sins (He had no sins of His own), His death must have been punishment on behalf of others. This is what the Bible clearly teaches. When Jesus hung on the cross, under the punishment of death, He hung there for sinners. This is the Christian gospel. Gospel means *good news.* The Christian good news is that Jesus died for sinners. God the Father punished His Son in your place or on your behalf. The sin of sinners has been punished in the person of Jesus Christ. Consider carefully the following texts, which say that Jesus died for sin and sinners.

1. 1 Peter 3:18 (NT) According to this verse, what did Jesus die for? _____

To whom does the term *righteous* refer?

_____

To whom does the term *unrighteous* refer?

_____

What does *righteous* mean? (If you forgot, look back to Lesson Two)

_____

_____

_____

_____

For whom did Christ die?

_____

When most people think about the cross of Jesus Christ, they think of the immensity of God's love. Jesus loved people so much that He was willing to suffer the punishment of sin, even though He never sinned during His entire time on earth. The cross of Christ symbolizes the greatest love in the world. While the cross certainly does signify the greatest love, it also signifies the greatest wrath and judgment of God, as well. Just think about it, God hates sin so much that He would require His one and only Son to be nailed on a cross, for others to be set free. The crucifixion was the darkest hour in human history. Jesus Christ, who created the whole world, was nailed to a cross by those very people He created. What utter humiliation!

When Jesus was nailed to the cross, God the Father poured out His wrath on God the Son. All the sins of the world were placed on Jesus. Our sin was on Him that dark day 2,000 years ago. His death was vicarious (on our behalf). If God did not become man, He could not have been crucified on the cross. God became man, for the purpose of paying for people's sin.

2. The character of God is such that He must judge sin. His holiness requires it. The atonement (payment of sin) of Jesus Christ was not only sufficient to cover the sins of the whole world, it was also sufficient to satisfy the wrath of God against sin. Please explain what Christ's death on behalf of sinners has to do with God's wrath.

_____

_____

_____

_____

3. Romans 4:25 (NT) According to this verse, Jesus died for whose sins?

_____

_____

_____

_____

Copy the first nine words of verse 25 and take time to meditate upon them.

_____

_____

_____

_____

What do these first nine words of verse 25 mean to you, as you consider your own sins?

_____

_____

Take time to list some of your sins that come to mind at this time.

_____

_____

_____

_____

Was Jesus delivered over to death for these, according to Romans 4:25? _____

4. Romans 5:6 (NT) Are you ungodly?

_____

Did Christ die for you?

_____

Did Christ die for righteous people, people without sin?

_____

Sometimes Satan deceives people into thinking they must better themselves, or give up all their sins, or begin to obey God before God will accept them. This is deception. Romans 5:6 says, *Christ died for the ungodly*, not the perfect person.

5. Romans 5:8 (NT) Whom did Christ die for?

_____

6. Hebrews 2:9 (NT) Whom did Jesus taste death for?

_____

It should be plain that Jesus' death was not an accident, nor was it for His own sins. His death was planned from eternity. He died a vicarious, substitutionary death on behalf of sinners. He died in the place of the ungodly, the unrighteous, and the impure. He died in the place of homosexuals, lesbians, adulterers, murderers, thieves, liars, tax cheaters, gossips, swearers, slanderers, grudge-holders, you and me.

Lesson SEVEN

THE BURIAL AND RESURRECTION OF CHRIST

Jesus Christ was God in human flesh. He gave His own life on behalf of sinners. The sins of mankind have been paid for in the person of Jesus Christ. Since the penalty of sin is death, Jesus suffered that punishment in His own body and soul. He died! Equally true, and just as important, is the gospel of truth that Jesus did not remain dead. All human beings who have ever died, millions upon millions, remain dead even now. But such is not the case with Jesus Christ. He died—then rose again on the third day. This truth is vital to Christianity. It is just as plainly revealed in the Holy Scriptures as Jesus' death.

Let's consider first what happened to Jesus' body between the crucifixion and the resurrection.

I. THE BURIAL OF JESUS CHRIST

1 Corinthians 15:1-4 (NT) According to verse 1, what did Paul declare to the Corinthians?

_____

_____

_____

_____

According to the very first phrase of verse 2, what does this gospel do for people?

_____

_____

_____

_____

In your own words, what does saved mean?

_____

_____

_____

_____

The gospel saves people! Through the gospel, people are delivered, rescued, or spared punishment from their sins and sin's penalty—death. According to verse 3, is the gospel of secondary importance? Why do you think we are studying the gospel in these lessons?

_____

_____

_____

_____

Since Paul says the gospel is of first importance, would you consider a preacher to be a true preacher, or a church to be a true church, if their emphasis was not placed upon the gospel? Why or why not?

_____

_____

_____

_____

The gospel is foundational to Christianity. In fact, the gospel is Christianity! According to verses 1-4, (Keep in mind, Paul is reminding these people of the gospel in verse 1.) what are the three parts of the gospel?

_____

_____

_____

_____

The burial of Jesus Christ was the link between His death and His resurrection. His burial substantiated His certain death. According to Matthew 12:40, how long was Jesus buried?

_____

_____

_____

_____

Stop and think about a burial today. Why do we bury people who have died? A burial is for several reasons. (1) It is the definite guarantee of death. Burial proves death. Jesus' death was likewise proven by His burial. (2) It is the removal of that which is unclean and decaying. Jesus was removed, because He was dead and unclean. He had died. Dead people are buried. Take the time to read Matthew 27:32-66. Some of these verses describe Jesus' burial. (3) Jesus Christ did not remain in the tomb. He was miraculously resurrected. Remember, according to 1 Corinthians 15:1-4, the resurrection of Christ is part of the gospel. There is no gospel without the resurrection.

2 Timothy 2:8 (NT) According to this verse, is the resurrection part of the gospel?

_____

Write down the portion of the verse that supports your answer.

_____

_____

Matthew 12:40 (NT) The phrase Son of Man refers to Jesus Himself. (Son of Man is used over 80 times in the Gospels and it always refers to Jesus). In this verse, Jesus alludes to His burial in the grave, or in the heart of the earth. From this verse, how do you know Jesus would rise again?

What is the time limit Jesus places upon His time in the grave?

Some have wondered: If Jesus was in the grave for three days and three nights, how could he rise the third day? The simple answer to the legitimate question is taken from Jewish culture. The Jewish calendar and rendering of days is not completely equivalent to ours. Several passages bearing this out are Genesis 42:17-18; 1 Samuel 30:12-13; 1 Kings 20:29; 2 Chronicles 10:5; Esther 4:16, 5:1)

Go back to 1 Corinthians 15:1-4 again. Did Jesus rise after three days?

Matthew 20:17-19 (NT) Who does the Son of Man refer to in verse 18? What does Jesus say will happen to the Son of Man?

(Take time to read Matthew 27:1-56 and see if these verses came true).

In Matthew 20:18, where does Jesus say all of these cruelties will take place?

_____

John 2:18-22 (NT) What sign does Jesus promise to perform to prove His authority?

_____

What did Jesus mean by, *destroy this temple*?

_____

How long did Jesus say it would be before He would rise again?

_____

Matthew 28:6 (NT) What does the angel affirm as to Jesus' whereabouts?

_____

Ephesians 1:20 (NT) What does Paul say that God the Father did to God the Son, Jesus Christ?

_____

Hebrews 13:20 (NT) What phrase in this verse teaches the resurrection of Christ?

_____

1. 1 Peter 3:18 (NT) According to this verse, what did Jesus do for our sins? Did He remain dead?

_____

How do you know?

_____

Look up each of the following verses. See how important the doctrine of the resurrection was in the preaching and teaching ministry of the early church. (All in the book of Acts) Acts 2:22-24; 3:13-15; 4:10,33; 10:39-40; 13:26-31; 17:1-3; 26:22-23

What is the significance of Jesus' resurrection? What does His resurrection mean to mankind?

_____

_____

_____

_____

The resurrection of Christ is important for at least four reasons.

RESURRECTION OF CHRIST MEANS THE PENALTY OF SIN (DEATH) HAS BEEN CONFRONTED AND TRIUMPHED OVER

You will recall from Lesson Three, there are three types of death spoken of in the Scriptures.

A. Spiritual Death: Separation of man from God due to sin (Genesis 2-3; Ephesians 2:1; Revelation 3:1; Matthew 8:18-22; Colossians 2:13; John 5:25; 1 Timothy 5:1-6). All men are born into this world spiritually dead.

B. Physical Death: Separation of the soul and body (Genesis 5; Matthew 10:28; James 2:26).

C. Eternal Death: Separation of the soul and body from God in the Lake of Fire (Luke 16:19-31; Revelation 20:11-15).

1. 2 Timothy 1:8-10 (NT) According to verse 10, what has Jesus done to death?

_____

If Jesus had remained in the grave, would death have been destroyed? Why or why not?

---

2. Revelation 1:18 (NT) Who holds the keys of death now?

Keys show ownership. You possess keys to your house and car, because you own them. Likewise, I possess keys to my house and car, because I own them. Jesus possesses the key of death, because He owns death. Death bowed to Jesus at His resurrection.

THE PHYSICAL, BODILY RESURRECTION OF CHRIST GUARANTEES THE   RESURRECTION OF ALL WHO ARE UNITED TO HIM THROUGH FAITH

The Scriptures plainly teach that all men, Christian and non-Christian, will rise from the grave. John 5:28-29 says, *Marvel not at this: for the hour is coming, in the which all that are in the graves shall hear his voice, And shall come forth; they that have done good, unto the resurrection of life; and they that have done evil, unto the resurrection of damnation..* The good and the evil will rise again. That includes all men. But the evil will rise (this includes all who fail to trust Christ as Savior) only to be condemned to death again (eternal death). Not so for the righteous (this includes all who have been forgiven of their sins). The Christian will rise again to live forever throughout eternity in the presence of God. It is Jesus' own resurrection from the dead that guarantees the Christian's resurrection from the dead.

1. 1 Corinthians 15:20-23 (NT) Notice the word *firstfruits* in verse 20. In our day, we rarely use this word, because most of us do very little farming. In agriculture, the first fruits are the very first samples picked from the crop. The first fruits indicate there is more of the crop to come later. Likewise, Paul says in verse 20 that Jesus' resurrection was the *firstfruits* of those who have fallen asleep. It is Paul's way of saying that there are more resurrections to come. Paul is speaking of the certainty of the Christian's resurrection, a resurrection just like Jesus'! In verse 23, Paul says in effect that when Christ comes again, all who belong to Him will rise again.

2. 1 Thessalonians 4:13-14 (NT) The Christians to whom Paul was writing were excessively grieving over the loss of their loved ones. Some of their Christian relatives and church members had physically died. The survivors were thinking they would never again see their loved ones. But Paul tells them in verse 13 not to be ignorant of the fact that Jesus' own resurrection guaranteed all Christians' resurrections. This, Paul plainly spells out in verse 14. *For if we believe that Jesus died and rose again, even so them also which sleep in Jesus will God bring with him.* Paul is plainly stating Jesus' resurrection guarantees the resurrection of all who belong to Him (Christians).

What, then, is it that certifies your resurrection?

_____

Do you fear physical death?

_____

If so, what do you fear about it?

_____

The Bible does not teach reincarnation. The Bible does guarantee resurrection. There is a big difference in the two. Reincarnation is based upon the myth that men will return in a subsequent life in a different form. Resurrection teaches that Christians will physically, bodily rise as the same person.

THE RESURRECTION OF CHRIST GIVES THE CHRISTIAN A NEW STANDING BEFORE GOD. GOD NOW SEES THE CHRISTIAN AS BEING SIN FREE.

When Christ rose from the dead, God the Father was in essence giving a receipt to the world, saying He was satisfied with the payment paid for sin. Had the Father not been satisfied with the offering of Christ for our sins—had the payment been insufficient—Jesus would have remained in the grave. But the Father lifted the Son from death, because the payment was sufficient—the sin-debt had been paid in full. See 1 Corinthians 15:17 (NT) According to this verse, if Christ did not rise from the dead, what would be true of Christians? _____ But since Christ has risen from the dead, are we still in our sins? _____

This verse is talking about how God views us once we are saved. It is not talking about our daily experience. Once we are saved by placing faith in Christ, God views us differently. We are given a new standing before Him. We are no longer guilty as sinners, but forgiven of all sins—hence, we are not still in our sins. In our daily experiences, we do still struggle with sin, but those sins are not put to our account. Rather, Jesus suffered for them, too.

1. 1 Peter 1:3-5 (NT) Accordingly to vs 3, what has God given us?

_____

How did God give us this new birth?

_____

Jesus died for our sins. He carried our sins to the cross. He suffered the penalty of sin (death). But He rose again! At His resurrection, He left all of our sins behind. Our sins are no longer charged to Him. Since He died for me and I believe in Him, His resurrection was also for me. In God's eyes, His resurrection gave me a new birth, a spiritual birth where God now sees me as a new creation. 2 Corinthians 5:17 says, "Therefore, if anyone is in Christ (in Christ always means attached to Him through faith), he is a new creation; the old has gone, the new has come! "Sin is now behind the Christian. It was placed behind him at Christ's resurrection. It took effect for each sinner when He first placed faith in Christ as Savior and Lord. Take time to read 1 Peter 1:21-25. These verses also speak of the Christian's new birth. Take time also to read 1 Thessalonians 4:13-18; John 5:28-29, 11:17-26; 1 Corinthians 15:12-58.

THE RESURRECTION OF JESUS CHRIST IS FOUNDATION TO THE GOSPEL

Some people reject believing in the resurrection because it allows them to reject the person of Jesus Christ. If they were to admit the resurrection, they would also have to admit Jesus was God. This, of course, would require submission to Christ. Some people place reason as their ultimate source of authority regarding what they believe, and they say the resurrection does not make logical sense (remember lesson one, the four sources of authority people use to determine truth). "People do not come back to life after being in the grave for days." Others place experience as their final authority, and if they have not seen it themselves, they will not believe it. "If Jesus would appear to me in His resurrected body, then I may believe in Him." Let's look at one final passage where Jesus dealt with this very issue even with one of His original twelve apostles. John 20:19-31 Read this account. Jesus appears to His disciples the very day of His resurrection, that Sunday evening. All of the apostles were there, except Thomas. Later, the apostles went to Thomas to inform Him Jesus had risen from the dead, and He appeared to them in His resurrected body. Thomas doubts this reality. What is Thomas' response according to verse 25?

Lesson EIGHT

GOD'S COMMAND IS FOR ALL PEOPLE TO REPENT AND BELIEVE THE GOSPEL

Having understood that Jesus Christ paid the penalty for man's sins and that the resurrection was God's statement that He was satisfied with the payment made, you might be wondering, "Why doesn't everyone go to heaven then?" In other words, if Jesus made sufficient payment for sins (and He did!) why will people end up in Hell? (Matthew 7:13-14) How can this be, or why is this, since Jesus already paid for the sins of sinners? The Scriptures are plain that God does not freely bestow salvation upon every sinner. Those who partake of God's salvation, found only in Jesus Christ, must receive this offer from God through repentance and faith.

I. REPENTANCE IS ESSENTIAL FOR SALVATION

Everyone likes a good deal. We all look for sales on groceries, clothing, furniture, etc. We want to get something good with little investment on our part. This is the way it is with salvation. Many sinners desire to *get in on a good deal* without any sincerity on their part. Many want to miss hell, but they refuse to come to God His way, as written in the Bible. God says in the Scriptures that men must repent and believe, if they are to receive God's free salvation. In your opinion, what does the word *repent* mean?

_____

_____

_____

_____

The following are three definitions of the word *repent* or *repentance* given by reputable Bible scholars. See if your definition agrees.

a) Turning from sin, we denominate REPENTANCE—T.P. Simmons

b) Repentance is a change of mind concerning one's obligation to the will and word of God—Emery Bancroft

c) Repentance is essentially a change of mind—Thiessen

Even Webster's New World Dictionary defines the term repent as *to feel such regret, as to change one's mind.* It should be plain that repentance (or to repent) means to change one's mind about his or her sin. Knowing now the meaning of repentance, look up and read each of the following verses speaking of repentance. Matthew 3:1-2; Matthew 4:17; Mark 6:12; Luke 24:45-47; Acts 2:38; Acts 17:30; Acts 20:21; Acts 26:20

1. Which text above shows that Jesus Himself preached repentance?

_____

Knowing Jesus preached repentance and realizing the definition of repentance, what then did Jesus encourage sinners to do?

_____

2. Which of the above texts shows that John the Baptist believed in repentance?

_____

3. Which of the above texts show what Peter did?

_____

4. Having read the texts above, did Jesus ever send His chosen twelve out to preach? Did He command them to preach that people should change their mind about their sin? What text proves this?

_____

5. Looking at Mark 6:6-13, what did Jesus enable the twelve to do—what miraculous gifts?

_____

_____

_____

_____

Isn't it interesting that healing the sick and driving out unclean demons was not enough? That only solved men's physical problems. There was something far more important—man's spiritual problems. Jesus commanded the twelve to preach repentance. Even today, so many want their physical problems cured, but care very little about their sinful soul.

6. Did the Apostle Paul preach repentance to people?

_____

How do you know?

_____

7. According to Acts 17:30-31, who does God command to repent?

_____

Come the Day of Judgment, will God judge men as to whether they have repented?

_____

Repentance in the Bible can be described as basically three things:

a) Conviction of sin (This is where a person is confronted with the truth and is convinced he has gone astray from that truth in his life.)

b) Confess sin to God

c) Willingness to turn from sin and desire a change in behavior.

Please read Acts 8:9-23. Why do you think Peter commands Simon to repent in verse 22?

_____

_____

_____

_____

In Acts 8:9-23, we read of a very wicked man named Simon the Sorcerer. Through the preaching of the Apostles, he purportedly believed in Jesus and got saved. (See Acts 8:13.) Only a few verses later, though, we read Peter declared Simon to still be unsaved. In verse 20, Peter speaks of Simon as one who will perish. In verse 22, Peter commands Simon to repent. In verse 23, Peter informs Simon he is *captive to sin*—obviously, a statement true only of an unsaved person. Nevertheless, Simon had *believed* in Jesus according to Acts 8:13. Obviously, his faith was not genuine saving faith, but a counterfeit faith. He did not come to God with a repentant heart. Subsequent church history bears out that Simon went on to become a great persecutor of Christians.

What is referred to here is the true faith of Christ. Simon was not a Christian. It is remarkable that Peter judged him so soon, when he had seen but one act of his. But it was an act satisfying him that he was a stranger to the faith. One act sometimes brings out the whole character. It may represent the governing motives. It may show traits of character utterly inconsistent with true faith. Then it is as certain a criteria as any long series of acts. There is no evidence here Peter saw this in a miraculous manner, or by any supernatural influence. It was apparent and plain, Simon was not influenced by the pure, disinterested motives of the Gospel, but by the love of power and of the world in the sight of God. That is, God sees or judges that your heart is not sincere and pure. **No external profession is acceptable without the heart.**

Reader, is your heart right with God? Are your motives pure? Does God see there the exercise of holy, sincere, and benevolent affections toward Him? God knows the motives—and with unerring certainty He will judge, and with unerring justice He will fix our doom according to the affections of the heart. Repent, therefore. Here we may remark: 1) Simon was at this time an unconverted sinner; 2) the command was given to him as such; 3) he was required to do the thing; not to wait or seek merely, but to actually repent; 4) this was to be the first step in his conversion. He was not even directed to pray first. His first indispensable action was to repent; that is, to exercise proper sorrow for his sin, and to abandon his plan or principle of action. 1) This shows that all sinners are to be exhorted to repent, as their first action. They are not to be told to wait, and read, and pray in the expectation repentance will be given them. 2) Prayer will not be acceptable or heard, unless the sinner comes repenting: that is, unless he regrets his sin and desires to forsake it. Then, and only then, will he be heard. When he comes loving his sins, and resolving still to practice them, grieved that he is guilty, and feeling his need of help, God will hear his prayer. See Isa. 1:15; Micah 3:4; Prov. 1:28; Ps. 96:18. Having a desire to forsake the sin, and to be pardoned, then pray to God to forgive, it would be absurd to ask forgiveness until a man felt his need of it; this shows a sinner ought to pray, and how he ought to do it, it should be with a desire and purpose to forsake sin, and in that state of mind God will hear the prayer. (Albert Barnes, Barnes Notes, Acts pg. 115, underline added.)

Repentance is not only to be a mark of the believer, where he is frequently being convicted of sin and turning from it, it is necessary when it comes to salvation. If a person desires to place his faith in Jesus Christ, it must come through a repentant heart and a willingness to turn from his sinful lifestyle. The operative word here is *willing*. You do not need to make changes in your life to come to Christ, but if you are genuinely repentant, the change will follow. The change that needs to take place is in the heart. Repentance has to do with a change in heart regarding sin. Make no mistake about it—without repentance, there is not true conversion.

Many people leave out the necessity of repentance in salvation. They say it is adding to faith alone. This is precisely why you have people supposedly getting saved, but there is never a change in their life. Those people say they do have faith and the way they live was never part of the *forgiveness and heaven deal*. People told me that I just had to believe, nothing was said about a willingness to change.

It is crystal clear from the teaching of Jesus and from the rest of Scripture, there is no salvation without repentance. When you communicate the gospel to others and the need to be saved, never leave out the necessity of repentance. You want to communicate a biblical gospel, not an incomplete and false gospel. Conversion and forgiveness come through repentance and faith in Christ.

II. FAITH IN CHRIST IS ESSENTIAL FOR SALVATION

There are literally hundreds of verses teaching faith in Jesus Christ as essential for salvation. Faith in Jesus Christ is the cornerstone of Christianity. Without faith in Christ, it is impossible to know God. What is saving faith? Scripture repeatedly states that men are freely saved by placing their faith in Jesus Christ. Scripture also informs us that some have believed in Jesus, but have not been saved. In other words, there is such a thing as counterfeit faith.

Consider James 2:19. This verse informs us that the demons (fallen angels) believe in God! Again, it is obvious they aren't saved. Their faith is not a saving faith. What then is genuine saving faith? Can it be defined? It sure can. It is important to note that the word *believe* in the Bible carries with it more than just the idea of intellectual agreement. When the Bible says all you need to do is *believe in Jesus*, it is not merely saying that all you need to do is agree that Jesus is the Son of God. It carries with it the idea of relationship. This is why many people, who say they believe in Jesus and think they are going to heaven, are still lost. They do not understand that *believe* in the Bible carries with it more than just the idea of acknowledgment. What they mean by *believe* is different from what the Scriptures mean by *believe*.

Saving faith, the faith required to take a man to heaven, is comprised of three essential elements. If any of these three elements are missing, saving faith does not exist (nor does biblical belief). Those three elements are:

1) Knowledge   2) Assent   3) Trust

Look up Romans 10:17 (NT) According to this verse, what does faith come from?

_____

_____

_____

_____

1. A person must hear the message of Christ. In other words, knowledge must be acquired. If a person has no knowledge of his sinful condition before God or no knowledge of Christ's death for him, obviously such an individual cannot place his faith in Christ. One can only believe in an object he knows something about.

2. Look up Romans 10:9-10 (NT). What must be done with a person's mouth in order to be saved?

_____

To confess the Lord Jesus means to assent He is who He claims to be. After acquiring knowledge of Christ as the Son of God (Who came into the world to be punished for sinners), one must assent or agree he believes this. Knowledge of Christ is not enough. Many people possess knowledge of the one who lived in history named Jesus. Many have been taught Bible stories about Jesus. But they have never personally assented or agreed that the Bible's testimony of Jesus is true and reliable. There must, first of all, be knowledge of Christ. But one must confess that knowledge himself—meaning, one must assent for himself that such knowledge is true.

3. Since knowledge is absolutely essential for saving faith, what must you do or what is your responsibility to your unsaved friends, family, and workmates?

_____

4. Can an individual know all the facts of Christianity, be able to recite hundreds of Bible verses, and accurately communicate the plan of salvation, yet be unsaved?

_____

Why?

_____

_____

_____

_____

5. One of the number one beliefs people have in this world, and particularly in this country, is that good people (those that are kind and loving) go to heaven and bad people (murderers and rapists) go to Hell. Is this an accurate statement? Explain and give Scripture for your answer.

_____

_____

_____

_____

Please take the time to read each of the following passages of Scripture, showing that for an individual to be saved, faith in Christ as Savior is essential: John 1:12-13; John 3:15-16; John 3:18; John 5:24; John 6:40; John 8:24; John 20:31.

As we have seen, God's command for every person is to repent and believe in the Gospel. Repentance has to do with a change in mind regarding sin, always resulting in a change in behavior. God does expect one to change their mind regarding sin. A change in behavior will be the fruit or result of their repentance—and that will be seen after salvation. The repentance that happens at conversion is 1) a conviction of sin—that one has in fact rebelled against God through his sin, 2) a confession of this to God, 3) a willingness to change. If a person is not willing to leave their life of sin, they do not display a truly repentant heart. Therefore, they are not accepting God's salvation. God's command is repent and believe. With a repentant heart, one places his faith personally in the Lord Jesus Christ. This is by knowledge, assent, and personal trust. At this point one is converted and becomes a child of God. This is true conversion.

There is no other way to God, apart from repentance and faith in Jesus. God has established the criteria. It is nothing more than repentance and faith—and it is certainly nothing less. At salvation, one's sins are forgiven and Heaven will await him/her at death. How gracious and loving God is, that He is willing to grant us forgiveness through faith in Jesus Christ.

To God is the glory!

Lesson NINE

THE FRUITS OF TRUE CONVERSION TO CHRIST

Some people claim to be Christians, but their lives do not show any marked difference after their supposed conversion. They seemed to be genuine when they made their profession to believe in Jesus Christ, and they seemed to have a repentant heart. They said they became a Christian, but that was many years ago, and their lives are not much different than they were before their supposed salvation. Perhaps they responded to an altar call, or engaged in the *sinner's prayer* years ago or when they were a child, or possibly they have an intellectual belief in Jesus. The problem, however, is there is not much difference between their lives and those in the rest of the world. There is not a hunger for God, a life different than the world, or a desire to grow spiritually. What does the Bible have to say about such a one?

Do you know someone fitting into the category described above? Perhaps you have a friend or relative claiming to be a Christian, but there is no hunger for the person of Jesus Christ. Maybe you are that person described above. Whether this lesson is describing you, someone you know, or no one you presently are aware of, this lesson is important for you to understand. The Biblical principle we will look at this lesson has become a major point of ignorance in many of our churches today. Is a person making a profession or confession to make Jesus Christ his/her Lord definitely saved and going to heaven—no matter what they do after that profession? Can a person verbally decide to make Jesus Christ his personal Savior, but have no change of life, show no fruits of repentance, live exactly the same as before, for years and years, and yet still go to Heaven? Can a person get saved and be forgiven and yet never grow? All of these questions are very important to answer, because if the answer is *no*, there are many people holding a false sense of security and will be tragically surprised on the Day of Judgment.

Do the Scriptures answer these crucial questions? Yes, they do! If you were to ask these hard questions to the average church goer, more than likely they would respond by saying, "Yes, it is possible to be saved and yet not show it outwardly in life." Most of the time the titles given to this type of person are a carnal Christian, a backslidden Christian, or a Christian who was never in an environment where he could grow. What do the Scriptures say about this hotly debated and often sensitive issue?

1. Carefully read Matthew 13:1-9, 18-23. In this passage, Jesus is comparing the seed in farming with the seed of the Word of God. The produced crop is analogous to the change of behavior due to conversion. There are four scenarios. The first scenario is in verse 19. Explain in your own words the main obstacle preventing this person from receiving the gospel.

_____

_____

_____

_____

The third scenario is in verse 22. There is a reason for going to scenario three before two. Explain in your own words the main obstacle here.

_____

_____

_____

_____

The second scenario is in verses 20-21. This is the one you want to pay close attention to. Read it carefully. In this scenario does the person receive the Word?

_____

How does he receive the Word? What does this mean?

_____

_____

_____

_____

Does he show any fruit at first? How long does it last? What happens, however, when persecution or problems come along?

_____

_____

_____

_____

How would you explain this scenario in your own words?

_____

_____

_____

_____

The fourth scenario is in verse 23. How would you describe this in your own words?

_____

_____

_____

_____

What is the difference between this fourth scenario and the other three?

_____

_____

_____

_____

Which of these would be someone who has truly been converted and saved? What does Jesus communicate as to the criteria of making this evaluation?

_____

_____

_____

_____

It is clear, Jesus communicates several different scenarios in the context of what someone does with the issue of the Gospel. Some do not understand the Gospel, thus cannot be saved (Seed 1). Some understand it, but they are too preoccupied with the cares of the world. They are more interested in this life, than the life to come (Seed 2). Some understand the Gospel and even receive it with joy, and perhaps make a profession of faith, but soon the depth of their faith is shown by a lack of fruit and falling away (Seed 3). This is interesting, because someone can actually receive the message, and accept it for a time, but actually not be genuinely converted. This means, some that engage in a sinner's prayer ask Jesus to be their Savior, or respond to an invitation, can actually still be lost. The issue is their heart has not been changed. If their heart has not been changed by conversion, it will eventually come out in real life.

Those that have honestly engaged in repentance and personal faith in Jesus, they are the ones truly saved and will bear fruit. Listen to what one Bible scholar says about these false conversions:

"Jesus explains this as denoting those who hear the gospel; who are caught with it as something new or pleasing; who profess to be greatly delighted with it, and who are full of zeal for it. Yet they have no root in themselves. They are not true Christians. Their hearts are not changed. They have not seen their guilt and danger, and the true excellence of Christ. They are not really attached to the gospel; and when they are tried and persecution comes, they fall—as the rootless grain withers before the scorching rays of the noonday sun." (Albert Barnes, Barnes Notes. Matt. Pg. 142-3).

It is clear. It is possible to profess Christ, to receive the gospel with joy, to acknowledge Jesus as Savior, and yet be completely lost and still under God's wrath. The issue is not what comes out the mouth, the issue is what comes out of both the <u>mouth and heart</u> (look up Romans 10:9-10 for this distinction). The heart manifests itself in actions and behavior. This is, of course, the fruit of outgrowth of the heart. A heart that is converted and changed will be demonstrated outwardly in life. (A note of caution: This principle of fruit signifying true conversion can be taken further than the Scriptures teach and can turn into a works salvation, i.e., you are saved by your fruits or works alone.)

That would be taking this theological principle too far and would be extremely dangerous. A person is not saved by what he does. A person is saved by placing his/her faith in Jesus Christ. If someone has truly done that, the result or outgrowth of that will be a changed heart and life. Faith is the foundation of forgiveness and conversion; fruit and deeds are the confirmation. No one can earn salvation by a changed life or by fruit. Deeds and fruit are always the result—faith is always the foundation.

2. Do you understand this important distinction between the foundation and conversion and the fruit of it? Explain it in your own words.

_____

_____

_____

_____

Let us now look at other passages teaching the principle that you cannot have genuine saving faith apart from the fruit of a changed life.

3. Please read James 2:14-26. Explain in your own words the message James is trying to get across.

_____

_____

_____

_____

The main issue in this passage is the relationship between a person's faith and his deeds (works, actions, fruit, life, etc.). What is the relationship between believing in something and how that belief is shown in everyday life? The word that is used for someone claiming to believe in something, yet contradicts that belief by his actions, is a _hypocrite_. If a person says he believes in Jesus Christ, and yet lives a life that contradicts His teachings, there is a question as to the genuineness of his belief. (Remember the definition for biblical belief.) Can a person have biblical faith in Jesus, yet not worship Him consistently in church, never seek Him through personal reading in the Bible, never talk about Him to others, never spend time in prayer, and live life like He is not even there? Is it possible to have a belief or faith in Jesus Christ and yet not produce a changed life or a life reflecting a living relationship with Christ? Although a person is not saved by his works, deeds, or fruit, is it possible to be saved without these things? This is the question raised in verse 14. Read this verse again.

What is the answer given to this question in verse 17?

_____

Many people claim to be Christians. In fact, most surveys suggest, at least 3/4 of people in this country are truly born-again. Why such a difference? The reason is two-fold: 1) People believe if they have good, Christian morals that makes them a Christian. 2) What most people mean when they say they are a Christian is they acknowledge the facts of Jesus Christ. They do not deny Jesus Christ and acknowledge He was who He said He was. Because of this intellectual assent or belief in Jesus, they feel this makes them a Christian.

As we saw, however, in the last lesson, an intellectual belief in Jesus is not enough. Repentance and personal trust in Jesus is also essential, which will always result in works of a changed life. A commitment to live for Jesus cannot be substituted for a mere intellectual acknowledgment of Him. People, however, say, "As long as I believe in God, He will forgive me. As long as I am not an atheist, God will not condemn me." Copy what James says in verse 19 in response to this statement.

_____
_____
_____
_____

James says that even the demons know God exists—even they have a fear of Him. If someone believes in God, does that mean he is saved and going to Heaven? Of course not. If that were the case, Satan and all his demons would be going to Heaven, because they certainly do not deny His existence. Most people believe in God's existence, but that is not sufficient for salvation.

How many times have you heard people say proudly they believe in God, suggesting this makes them okay spiritually?

_____

What is James' conclusion in verses 20-26?

_____

How is this passage reconciled with the passages by Paul emphasizing faith and not works? Many have concluded James and Paul contradict each other: James 2:24 says, *you see that a person is justified by what he does and not by faith alone*; Ephesians 2:8-9 says, *For it is by grace you have been saved, through faith —and this not from yourselves, it is the gift of God—not by works, so that no one can boast.*

Although at first glance these two passages might seem to be contradicting each other, they are not. The biggest problem with people trying to put two verses side by side, showing the way they contradict each other, is the verses are taken out of context. Paul and James, in their environment, were dealing with two opposite issues. Paul was dealing with people trying to say the only way to be saved is by obeying certain commandments. He emphasized to them they could never obey enough commandments and further emphasized that it is through faith we are saved, not works or deeds.

James was dealing with the opposite end of the spectrum (different context). He was dealing with people that said they could be saved by their intellectual belief in God—and it did not matter if they followed it with their life. He communicated to them this type of faith is dead. It is not the kind of faith that saves. The only kind of saving faith is a faith that produces works and deeds. A person does not have a faith that saves him, if it does not produce a life of new obedience to the teaching of Jesus. Genuine, saving, Biblical faith will always produce fruit in a person's life. If there is no fruit, the conclusion is that there is no genuine faith. Faith without works is dead!

4. Please read 1 John 2:3-6. What is the point John is trying to get across in this passage?

_____

_____

_____

_____

According to verse 3, what will happen if we obey His commands?

_____

This verse is dealing with the issue of assurance of salvation. It does not say we will come to know God, if we obey His teachings—it says we will know that we have come to know Him. There is a difference. God is saying that we will have confidence that we have personally come to know Christ, if we obey His teachings. The conclusion is, if we do not obey His teachings, we have not come to know Him. Here again is the issue of life change and obedience being necessary to genuine conversion. They cannot be separated.

According to verse 4, what is the conclusion regarding someone claiming to be saved or a Christian and his/her life does not show it?

_____

_____

_____

_____

5. Please read 1 John 3:10. What is the criteria by which judgment is passed, as to whether a person is saved or not?

_____

The answer, of course, is not what they intellectually believe in. The answer revolves around looking at their life. This again points to fruit, deeds, and works.

6. Please read Matthew 7:17-20. How does Jesus say you will recognize people?

_____

_____

_____

_____

What will happen to those who do not produce the fruit of conversion according to verse 19?

_____

_____

_____

_____

Go back and reread the first three paragraphs of this lesson. Give an explanation of what you would tell someone who asked you these questions. Give Scripture to back up your answer.

_____

_____

_____

_____

There are many people in this country who believe they are Christians. They base their claim on a prayer they once said, an invitation they once responded to, or an intellectual belief in Jesus and the Bible. There is nothing wrong with any of these scenarios, as long as a genuine conversion has taken place. Genuine conversion can only be distinguished by looking at a person's life and fruit. If their life shows relatively no difference from the life before their supposed conversion, there are hard questions to be asked. It is important to note that God does not expect change overnight. God is very patient with new believers. We should not expect young Christians to make mature, spiritual decisions right away.

It takes time to grow and learn how to live for Jesus. Fruit may not be immediately present, but they will (if true conversion) eventually be present. God works His timing out in different ways in different people. The issue here is not perfection. Christians are still sinful and struggle with sin. They will never attain perfection, but there should be visible change. The Scriptures are crystal clear—no fruit or changed life—no conversion or salvation. Often people feel this type of teaching is judgmental. The common argument is, "How can you pass judgment as to who is saved and who is not? We do not know someone's heart; therefore, we do not really know who is a true Christian and who is not." While it is true, we cannot say for sure who is definitely converted and who is not, the Scriptures do teach there are fruits to look for, to point one way or the other.

This is what this whole lesson has been about. A few examples of these fruits are a hunger for God's Word, a desire for prayer, a desire to grow spiritually, a repentance from sin, a desire to fellowship with other believers, a desire to see others saved, a life that is different from the rest of the world, etc. Only God knows the heart, but these are the outward indications.

7. Please read 2 Corinthians 13:5. Explain in your own words what everyone has a responsibility to do.

_____

_____

_____

_____

8. Take the time to examine yourself. Would you say you are *in the faith* (truly converted)? Why? (If you do not think you are or not sure, write that down and give the reasons why. It is far better to be honest and work from there, than to try to be deceiving, because of embarrassment and continue to be lost.)

_____

_____

_____

_____

This may be the most important question you have ever asked yourself. If your answer is not a definite *yes*, God's offer of salvation is to you, today. Through repentance and personal faith in Jesus, you can be forgiven of your sins and be a converted Christian. Make that decision right now and begin your life as a new follower of Jesus Christ. Do not let another day go by lost and on your way to Hell. Jesus is calling you now. Go over this lesson many times if you have to. Conform your mind to a Biblical understanding of what a Christian is and what it is not. Seek to proclaim the Gospel to others—the Gospel that is not defined by the world or current Christian culture, but is defined by the founder Jesus Christ Himself. On Judgment Day, His definition is the only one that will matter. Seek a Biblical definition of true conversion and salvation.

Lesson TEN

COMPLETE FORGIVENESS AND FREEDOM FROM THOSE IN CHRIST

This is the concluding lesson of this 10 week Bible study. In these lessons I have tried to be completely honest and forthright about what God has communicated to us in His Word. The Scriptures and Jesus Himself speak strongly against sin and the consequences of it. This is why there was so much time spent on the nature of sin in the first section of this booklet. Those that have this foundational understanding of sin and all its terrible effects are the ones, more than anyone else, to appreciate and grow to love God's complete, unalterable forgiveness to those united to Jesus. In fact, it is impossible to come to Christ without an understanding of sin. It is impossible to understand the full extent of God's grace, mercy, and forgiveness without first understanding the wickedness of sin. The verse, *this is love: not that we loved God, but that He loved us and sent His son as an atoning sacrifice for our sins,* (1 John 4:10) takes on a whole new meaning, if the nature and depth of sin is comprehended and studied.

This lesson, therefore, will look at the result of those that do come to Jesus Christ through repentance and faith. The result is perhaps one of the most amazing concepts to those converted to Jesus Christ. The issue of the forgiveness of sins is the most glorious blessing God could ever give us, because its effects last for an eternity. Let us look at some passages telling us what God does to those that come to Christ.

Preliminary Question: Have you repented and placed your total faith and trust in Jesus?

Go back to Lesson Nine and reread the answer you gave on question eight. If you said you are not in the faith, is your answer the same today? If it is, write down what you believe is the reason for you not repenting and placing faith in Christ today. What do you think is preventing you from salvation in Christ?

_____

_____

_____

_____

1. In Romans 8:1-2, what is the result of those who are in Christ Jesus?

_____

_____

_____

_____

What are you set free from according to verse 2?

_____

What do you think it means to be set free from the law of sin?

_____

2. In Romans 5:1, what is the result of being justified through faith?

_____

Did you know that before your faith in Christ, the Scriptures say that you were an enemy of God?

_____

What do you think it means to now have peace with God?

_____

Hebrews 8:12—This passage deals with the blessings of the new covenant. When Jesus came, He brought the new covenant. What does God say He will do to those who accept Jesus in this new covenant? God says He will remember their sins no more. What He means here is not that He will literally forget a person's sins. What He is saying is that when it comes to Judgment Day, He will not count their sins against them. As far as judgment, God will remember those sins no more. What an awesome thought! The King of the Universe, the pure and holy God Who despises sin, says to those who are in Christ, it will be like He does not even remember they sinned. If you are in Christ, it will be like He has forgotten your sins, when it comes to you paying for them. Considering all the sins you have committed, this is phenomenal! This should send us to our knees in complete humility and honor.

What do you think about God remembering your sins no more?

_____

3. Please read Colossians 2:13. According to this verse, how much of our sin is forgiven if we are in Christ?

_____

Are there any sins, no matter how bad or how many times committed, that will not be completely forgiven by God? The amazing thing about God's forgiveness to the born-again believer is He forgives all of his sins, not just half or most. There is nothing more freeing than to know God has taken all a person's sins away. Go back to Lesson Two and write on this line every sin you have committed and wrote down in that lesson. Do not miss one. If there are any others you can think of now, write them too. (This is not something you have to read to your Christian friend, but complete this question.)

_____

_____

_____

_____

Spend a couple of minutes looking at those sins and thinking about how God has totally taken those sins away. Write down your thoughts regarding the truth that Jesus paid for every one of those sins on the cross. Consider that God has completely and exhaustively forgiven you of every one of them, knowing that on Judgment Day it will be like He has no memory of them.

4. Take time to read Psalm 103. Write out all the references to God's forgiveness.

_____

_____

_____

_____

According to verse 3, how many of your sins are forgiven?

_____

Explain in your own words what is meant by verse 12.

_____

_____

_____

_____

The all-encompassing love and forgiveness of God has no limit or bounds. It is infinite. It is hard to fathom that God has completely removed our transgressions. A transgression is another word for *sin or violation of the law*. God has removed every one of your violations of His moral law. He has even removed the transgressions you do not even remember making. To recall all of our sins would be impossible, for the list would be too great for us to create. Oh, the love of God, that He would remove every single transgression! He deserves our worship.

Please read Isaiah 1:18. This passage considers sins as red as scarlet. Imagine taking a dress shirt and soaking it in a deep red paint. Imagine taking it out of the paint and letting it dry for a week. That shirt would be completely ruined. The red paint would be throughout every fiber in the shirt, staining it forever. This is characteristic of your life before conversion. Sin has affected every fiber of your being. You were completely stained with no hope of ever being clean. Now imagine God touching the shirt—and the shirt automatically turning a stark, crisp, snow white. Nothing short of a miracle could do that to that stained shirt. That is what God has done to your life. He has made your sin and your whole personhood as white as snow, completely clean. God sees you without one stitch of red. He has wiped you clean. What does this verse motivate you to do with the rest of your life?

_____

_____

_____

_____

5. Please read Psalm 32. List the phrases mentioning the forgiveness of God.

_____

_____

_____

_____

This is one of the great passages mentioning the blessings the forgiven receive. Is there any other gift God could give to you that would be more of a blessing or would be of greater significance than partaking in the complete forgiveness of God? Explain your answer.

_____

_____

_____

_____

According to verse 11, what is the response of the psalmist to the notion of God forgiving him?

_____

_____

_____

_____

The greatest gift God could ever bestow upon a person is the gift of forgiveness. If you have been saved through repentance and faith in Jesus Christ, the Scriptures say your sins have been washed away. On Judgment Day, you will not have to pay for your sins with eternal punishment. Jesus has paid the price for you. Your sins were transferred to Him and He nailed them to the cross. They are taken care of— and do not need to be remembered again. This realization of what Jesus has done for you is what motivates you to show your love for Him by living out His teachings. You do not live for God now to earn brownie points, so He will forgive you again—you live for God, because of what He has done for you.

Your obedience for Him is a response, fruit, or result of your complete forgiveness, not a means to attain forgiveness. We will struggle with sin—and we will still fall. Although we are forgiven, we still have a sinful nature that we battle against. Spend a few minutes at the close of this lesson, thanking, adoring, and worshipping

God for the wonderful gift of forgiveness. This forgiveness is not something you earned, it is given to you because of the infinite, all encompassing, and unfathomable love of the Creator of the universe. This gift will personally affect you not only in this life, but in the billions of years to come.

If you have come to saving faith in Jesus Christ through this study, your next important step is baptism. Baptism should take place as soon after your conversion to Christ as possible. Ask your Pastor for information on baptism. If you are still outside of salvation, if you have not undergone a true conversion through repentance and faith, do not allow yourself to remain in this hardness of heart. You now have an understanding of your sin, the consequences of it, the love Jesus Christ has shown you, and the means to partake of eternal life and forgiveness.

Do not allow this knowledge of the truth to be tossed aside. Apply it to your heart today. Ignorance will never be your excuse from this day forward. Turn to Christ and live!

We will close with a quote from one of the most powerful preachers in the history of Christianity, Charles Haddon Spurgeon, *The harvest is past, the summer is ended, and we are not saved* (Jeremiah 8:20). NOT SAVED! Is this your mournful plight? Warned of the judgment to come, bidden to escape for your life, and yet at this moment not saved? You know the way of salvation—you read it in the Bible, you hear it from the pulpit, it is explained to you by friends, and yet you neglect it and therefore are not saved. You will be without excuse when the Lord shall judge the living and dead. The Holy Spirit has given more or less of His blessing upon the word which has been preached in your hearing, and the times of refreshing that have come from His Divine Presence, and yet you are without Christ. These hopeful seasons have come and gone—your summer and your harvest have past—and yet you are not saved. Years have followed one another into eternity, and your last year will soon be here. Youth has gone, manhood is going, and yet you are not saved. Let me ask you—Will you ever be saved? If the convenient time never has come, why should it ever come?

It is logical to fear that it may never arrive, and that, like Felix, you will find no convenient season till you are in hell. Oh, be thinking of what that hell is, and of the dreaded probability that you will soon be cast into it! Suppose you should die unsaved, your doom no words can picture. Oh, be wise, be wise in time. Then another year begins, believe in Jesus, Who is able to save to the uttermost. Consecrate these last hours to lonely thought. If by humble faith in Jesus deep repentance be wrought in you, all will be well. Oh, see to it that this year pass not away, and you an unforgiven spirit. Now, Now, NOW, believe and live. Escape for thy life; look not behind thee, neither stay thou in all the plain; escape to the mountain, lest thou be consumed. —C.H.S.

May God never let your conscience rest until you turn to Him. This is His desire for your life. (2 Peter 3:9) For the rest of you that have come to Christ, this will be the most exciting and possibly the most challenging time in your life. The Bible says you are a new creation. For our final passage of this study, copy 2 Corinthians 5:17.

_____

_____

_____

_____

Although you will have the same personality, in time, your thinking and desires will change. You will begin to develop a godly character. When you become *born-again*, as Jesus referred to it, you are a babe in Christ. It is as if your eyes have just been opened. You will learn how to make the Bible your final source of authority for what is right and wrong—what is truth and error. What do you think it now means to have the Bible as your final source of authority for what you believe (instead of reason, tradition, or experience)?

_____

_____

_____

_____

Spend time getting to know your new Savior Jesus Christ by reading the Bible on a consistent basis (start now in the NT). Reading the Bible, praying, and involvement in a good Bible-teaching church will be the foundation to your growth in Christ. You are forgiven! You are free! Jesus says in John 8:36, *So if the Son sets you free, you will be free indeed.* Jesus has **set you free**. Amen! Let us spend the rest of our earthly lives loving Him, for He certainly deserves our love. Fill the VOID! Jesus is the answer. **To God be the glory!**

Conclusion

When Christ surrendered His life on the cross for each of our lives, He took on all things that keep us from a relationship with Him. Fear, anger, hate, bitterness, worry, panic, anxiety, negativity, resentment, guilt, intimidation, torment, misery, frustration, stress, irritability, impatience, trepidation, tension, friction, grudges, offenses, jealously, unforgiveness, animosity, pressure, intolerance, pride, selfishness, addictions—all those things that keep us in bondage.

When Christ hung on the cross and died, He robbed us of all these things. He took all of them on Himself, so we would never have to experience them again. All these things belong to Him because this is what He sacrificed His life for. When we have any of these things operating in our lives, we cannot rise up to the place He has set aside for us. He wants these things back, so it is up to us to be willing to surrender them.

He paid a huge price for all these things and they do belong to Him. When we hold on to any of those things, we rob them from Jesus. He took them on Himself, so we could be free. All those things are part of the bondage we find ourselves in.

JESUS is the answer to the VOID in our hearts, but we try to fill it with the things of this world. Place Him on the throne of your heart. Allow Him to rule and guide your life from this day forward.

Obey what you know!

Pray as you go!

Read your Bible to grow!

**Praise God from who all
blessing flow!**

CPSIA information can be obtained
at www.ICGtesting.com
Printed in the USA
LVHW050000050323
740850LV00007B/104